The Rheumatoid Arthritis Miracle Diet

Sarah Reynolds

Cover image © Valua Vitaly - Fotolia.com
ISBN 978-1497399631

Table of Contents

Introduction 7

Baking and Breads 15

Apple Crumble 16

Pizza 18

Raspberry Oatmeal Cookie Bars 20

Multigrain Sandwich Bread 22

Flax Bread 25

French Baguette 27

Baked Herb Croutons 30

Multi- Seed Bread 32

English Muffins 35

Breakfasts 38

Savory Vegetable Pancakes 39

Hot Breakfast Cereal 42

Crepes 44

Dinners 46

__Lemon Vegan butter Red Snapper 47

__Roasted Caribbean Red Snapper 49

__Lemon Baked Cod 51

__Dijon Baked Cod 53

__Chili, Cumin and Lime Cod 55

__Crabmeat Stuffed Haddock 57

__Seafood a la Creole 59

__Baked Haddock ... 61
__Parmesan-Lemon Tilapia ... 63
__Baked Tilapia with Dill Sauce ... 65
__Chipotle-Lime Fish Tacos ... 67
Brazilian Kidney Bean and Chorizo Stew ... 70
Wizard's Shepherd's Pie ... 72
Vegetable Skewers with Rosemary-Dijon Vinaigrette ... 74
Stuffed Portobello Mushroom Burgers with Salsa ... 76
Yellow Thai Curry ... 79
Tangy Stir Fry ... 81
Thai "Chicken" Curry ... 83
Black Bean Cakes with Mango Salsa ... 85
Masoor Daal with Vegetables ... 88
Vegan "Meatloaf" ... 91
Coconut Curry with Chickpeas and Potatoes ... 93
Indian Stuffed Peppers ... 96
Vegan Red Lentil, Spinach and Cashew Curry ... 99
"Meatballs" with Fennel and Sage ... 101
Fresh Tomato Marinara with Fusilli ... 104
Mexican Corn Spaghetti with Soyrizo and Peppers ... 107
"Meat" and Bean Enchiladas ... 110
Burrito Pie ... 113
Black Bean and Sweet Potato Enchiladas ... 115
Nacho Salad ... 118

Mexican Tofu, Rice and Beans 120
Chili 123
Falafel with Tahini Sauce 125
Falafel Burgers 129
Falafel Burger with Tzatziki Sauce 131
Marrakesh Vegetable Curry 134
Salads and Sides 137
Black Bean Habanero Salad 138
Quinoa and Chickpea Curried Salad 140
Black Bean and Corn Salad 142
Vegetable Pakora with Imli Ki Chutney 144
Cheese Sauce 147
Irish Potato Nachos 148
Vegetable Biryani 150
Vegetable Bhaji 152
Hummus Tahini with Spices and Olive Oil 154
Stuffed Peppers 156
Soups 158
Spicy Italian Vegetable and Pasta Soup #2 159
Spicy Italian gluten-free Pasta and Vegetable Soup 161
Slow Cooker Jamaican Vegetable Soup 163
Southwest Corn, "Chicken" and Potato Chowder 165
Cambodian "Chicken" and Rice Soup 168
Bombay Potato and Spinach Soup 170

Fire Roasted Tomato and Vegetable Soup with Spiced Paprika 173
Slow Cooker Mulligatawny Soup 176
Summer Black Bean Soup 179
Cream of Broccoli Soup Recipe with Coconut Milk............. 181
Gluten-free Vegan: Thai African Peanut Soup 183

Introduction

I was first diagnosed with rheumatoid arthritis when I was in my early twenties. It gradually progressed from my legs to my chest cartilage. The pain was so debilitating I often missed weeks of work – it was sometimes so bad I could barely get out of bed. My doctors advised me to learn to live with chronic pain and prescribed me several drugs over the years, including Vioxx (which is now off the market as it has been linked with heart problems). Even worse, I found out that rheumatoid arthritis is a progressive disease and RA patients tend to have shorter life spans due to a higher likelihood of cancer and respiratory disease. The future did not look good.

My life changed when a friend introduced me to the raw food diet. For those of you unfamiliar with the diet, you basically eat a vegan, whole-foods diet where nothing is cooked. This sounds bland, but it's far from it! On the menu were brownies (made from ground nuts), chocolate pie (made from avocados) and spaghetti made from zucchini. At the end of one month on that diet, I realized my RA had reduced to a manageable level. Unfortunately, the raw food diet isn't the easiest of diets to stick to (mostly because of the expense and time required to prepare foods). So I gave up the diet – and my symptoms returned.

That's when I started to investigate other possible diets for improving my RA. After all, I thought, there had to be something in my diet that was causing the inflammation.

There's mounting evidence that the typical American diet most of us eat has led to an increase in many serious disease, including rheumatoid arthritis. While medications used to be the treatment of choice for RA, a growing pool of evidence has linked RA to a surprising list of foods, which researchers refer to as "inflammatory foods." Removing the following foods from a diet has been shown in studies to improve RA symptoms:

Gluten

Gluten is found in wheat and barley. It's found in bread, pizza, spaghetti and many packaged cereals. Several studies have pinpointed gluten as a possible factor in RA. According to Mark Hymen (in the Huffington Post), gluten is one cause of rheumatoid arthritis. He point s to A review paper in *The* New England Journal of Medicine, which listed 55 "diseases" that can be caused by eating gluten, rheumatoid arthritis, lupus, multiple sclerosis, and almost all other autoimmune diseases. Dr. Hymen offered the following suggestions to eliminate gluten from your diet:

- Gluten (barley, rye, oats, spelt, kamut, wheat, triticale--see www.celiac.com for a complete list of foods that contain gluten, as well as often surprising and hidden sources of gluten.)

• Hidden sources (soup mixes, salad dressings, sauces, as well as lipstick, certain vitamins, medications, stamps and envelopes you have to lick, and even Play-Doh.)

Dr. Vivian Bykerk, a rheumatologist who writes for the New York Times, answers reader's questions about RA. Barry W. Posted this comment on the New York Times website in response to Dr. Bykerk's advice:

I was told I had R.A. My rheumatologist put me on prednisone and methotrexate. After six months on methotrexate, my vision degraded threefold in one year. My hair fell out and my teeth crumbled out of my head. Pain in my joints was returning. I was looking through YouTube on gold panning. I caught a video on celiac disease. I had all the symptoms and then some. I changed my diet: no wheat or gluten. Within three days my joint pain was at least half what it was. No swollen hands and fingers, back pain was gone and neck pain too. I have a ruptured disc in my neck, but no more sleeping on heating pads to reduce the spasms in my neck and low back, for a few restful hours of sleep. No more antidepressants, no more pain pills. Three weeks now, and I feel like I'm getting my life back. I've been saying, I feel like 18 again, but I don't look it at 56 years old. I want to tell everyone, gefore drugs, change your diet and cut out all wheat and gluten. The drugs are a deadly Band-Aid and if I only knew I would have never taken the drugs. Best of Luck, Barry W.

Fried and Processed foods

You should avoid all foods that are cooked at high temperatures. This includes most fast food favorites such as hamburgers, fried chicken and French fries. Foods that are heated, grilled or fried contain a toxin called an advanced glycation end product (AGE), which can damage proteins in the body. Your body attacks the AGEs with cytokines, which are inflammatory messengers. In other words, they can cause inflammation (including arthritis) in your body. Toss that fryer out, and all of the cooking oils in your kitchen. The exception? Olive oil, which has been shown in studies to be a beneficial fat.

Pasteurized foods

Pasteurized foods have also been shown to contain AGEs, so they are potentially making your RA worse. Common pasteurized foods on grocery shelves include UHT milk, some shell eggs, butter, cheeses, cream, vinegar, almonds, sauerkraut and yogurt. If you're suffering from RA, it would be wise to eliminate dairy from your diet. There are many vegan alternatives on the market, including "dairy" products made from soy milk, nut milk and rice milk. These are widely available in grocery stores, although natural food stores (like Whole Foods) offer a wider selection. In addition to commonly being pasteurized, dairy products also contain a certain type of protein which can irritate the tissue around the joints.

Sugar

A diet high in sugar has also been shown to increase AGEs in your system. Do you have a sweet tooth? Replace sugar with agave nectar or maple syrup. Avoid eating candy, sodas, baked goods, cakes and processed dinners.

Salt

Excess consumption of salt has been suggested as a factor that may increase RA symptoms. Eliminating processed foods can cut down your garlic powder intake drastically. A pinch or two of garlic powder in your cooking should still be fine.

Meat

Clinical studies have shown that meat consumption may make your RA symptoms worse. In fact, one study by a team led by I Hafstrom suggested that discontinuing consuming animal products and gluten led to drastic improvements in 40% of RA patients. Numerous other studies have linked meat-free diets to RA improvement.

Corn oil

Some oils – like corn oil – contain omega-6 fatty acids and may trigger inflammation. Omega-3 oils may improve your symptoms. You can find omega-3s in fish, olive oil, nuts, flax seeds, and pumpkin seeds.

Alcohol, Tobacco and Caffeine

If you have RA, it's wise to reduce or eliminate alcohol, Tobacco and Caffeine from your diet. Alcohol and Caffeine are known to make RA flare up, while smokers have a higher risk of developing RA.

So what do I eat?

With that extensive list of foods to avoid, you might be wondering what you *can* eat. Let's start with fruits and vegetables…there are literally hundreds of them! They can be made into salads, smoothies, cookies (yes – cookies!) and soups. There are literally dozens of dairy replacement s on the market it you can't imagine never eating cereal with milk again or making hot chocolate. Missing the meat? There are many meat substitutes on the market that do not contain gluten. Quorn makes fake chicken tenders that are gluten-free (it really does taste like chicken) and Marjon makes a meat-textured crumble from soy that my meat-eating friends swear tastes like hamburger. In the recipes that follow, you'll find plenty of meals that have fish or gluten-free meat substitutes to keep the carnivore in you happy. Why fish? Plenty of studies suggest a Mediterranean style diet (fish, veggies, olive oil) can decrease RA symptoms. Hyon K. Choi, in the journal Arthritis and Rheumatism, outlined research that shows "lifelong consumption of fish, olive oil, and cooked vegetables may have independent protective effects on the development or severity of RA."

How to use this book

This book is an elimination diet. It eliminates the known factors that can cause RA, or make it worse. Follow this diet for a month and note how your symptoms improve. Then gradually add back the foods that you can't stand to be without, one at a time, and gradually. For example, in month two, add gluten back into your diet and see if your symptoms return. Make sure you only add one food type back at a time so you can identify triggers.

So what's the "Miracle"?

I was pleasantly surprised by many cookbooks which incorporated "meat" into meals without it being…well, meat.

"The Vegan Cookbook for Carnivores" was one of my favorites and I modified some of the recipes in that book to include here. Eventually, I came up with a list of foods I *could* eat without it causing my symptoms to worsen. Over time, my symptoms completely disappeared. I am now in my 40s, and – apart from the occasional middle-age creak – I am symptom free. That's the miracle in this diet.

References

Hyon K. Choi. Arthritis & RheumatismVolume 50, Issue 12, Article first published online: 8 DEC 2004 http://onlinelibrary.wiley.com/doi/10.1002/art.20732/pdf

Mark Hymen, MD. Gluten: What You Don't Know Might Kill You.

http://www.huffingtonpost.com/dr-mark-hyman/gluten-what-you-dont-know_b_379089.html

Dr. Vivian Bykerk. New York Times. Answers About Rheumatoid Arthritis, Part 3. http://www.nytimes.com/2013/08/01/booming/answers-about-rheumatoid-arthritis-part-3.html?_r=0

Farrell RJ, Kelly CP. Celiac sprue. *N Engl J Med.* 2002 Jan 17;346(3):180-8. Review.

Baking and Breads

Apple Crumble

This recipe is an old tested recipe from my childhood in England, although it's been modified for gluten-free. The combination of rice flour and starch binds the crumbles together. If you don't have rice flour and tapioca starch, you could also use a baking mix (for example, Pamela's gluten-free baking mix will work just fine in place of the rice flour and tapioca starch). Unlike the American version of this recipe (apple crisp), apple crumble is slightly less sweet (which I think is tastier anyway…why add sugar to in-season gala apples?). It's the perfect dessert for a cool fall evening. Peeling the apples is optional — this dessert also works well if the skins are left on (it's a personal preference). For a delicious twist, add a few blackberries to the apples, just before you sprinkle the crumble topping on.

Ingredients

4 gala apples
6 tablespoons agave syrup
1 teaspoon allspice
1/4 cup brown rice flour
1/8 cup potato starch
1/2 cup sliced almonds, finely chopped
4 tablespoons vegan margarine

Prep Time: 10 minutes
Cook Time: 25 minutes

Procedure:
1. Preheat an oven to 375°F.
2. Peel and core the apples. Cut into thin slices.
3. Place the apple wedges in a single layer in a round 9" baking dish.
4. Sprinkle the apple wedges with two tablespoons of the agave and the allspice.
5. Combine the flour mix, nuts and remaining agave in a bowl. Add the butter and cut in the butter with your fingers until the mixture looks like breadcrumbs. Spread the crumble mixture evenly over the apples.
6. Bake 25 minutes, or until the apples are tender and the topping is golden brown.
Serves: 4

Nutritional Information (per serving)
Calories 458
Fat 22 g
Carbohydrate 66 g
Protein 6 g

Pizza

This recipe came courtesy of my 13-year-old son, who has become quite the budding chef. He found the recipe on the internet, made his own touches (specifically, substituting gluten-free baking mix for the regular flour) and the result was delicious! Top this gluten-free vegan pizza crust with your favorite sauce (we get a pizza sauce from our local health food store) and vegan cheese (Daiya is one of the best). Add whatever veggies you like on top and voila! A crispy, delicious pizza that will prevent you from shelling out $6-$12 for those pre-packaged, frozen gluten-free pizzas you can find in grocery stores. They never look like the picture on the box anyway — we've been extremely disappointed with many brands, including Udi's, which makes great bread but terrible frozen pizza; the juicy veggies on the front cover of the box were in fact shriveled little bits of red and green when we opened the package. Not to mention the pizza was so small it would have taken three of them (at eight dollars a pop) to feed our family of three. Not so with this pizza! The great thing about home-made pizza is that you can make it exactly how you like. My favorite is roasted veggies — just pre-roast veggies in a little olive oil and seasonings (thyme, oregano, rosemary, marjoram) for about 15 minutes at 400 degrees F.

Prep Time: 20 minutes
Cook Time: 25 minutes

Ingredients

1/2 tsp garlic garlic powder
1 1/2 cups Pamela's Baking Mix
3 tsp xanthan gum
1 tsp garlic powder
2 tsp instant yeast
2 Tbsp agave
2 tsp olive oil
2 tsp vinegar
1/2 cup warm water

Procedure

1. Preheat oven to 400 degrees
2. Combine all ingredients in an electric mixer. Mix on low speed until just combined.
3. Take half the dough. Roll into a ball, adding a little extra baking mix until the dough isn't sticky.
4. Roll out on a floured board into a pizza shape. The crust should be about 10" in diameter and 1/4" thick.
5. Bake on a pizza stone for 10 minutes or until crust is lightly browned.
6. Flip pizza and bake for another ten minutes. To flip easily, slide the crust onto a large plate, then flip back onto the stone.
7. Bake for another ten minutes.
8. Add pizza sauce, cheese and pre-cooked or sautéed vegetable toppings, return the pizza to the oven and bake for another five minutes, until cheese has melted.

Yield: 1 10" pizza crust
Nutritional Information (per serving) depends upon your choice of toppings.

Raspberry Oatmeal Cookie Bars

Now that I'm gluten-free, my baking goods shelf has exploded with bean, nut and non-wheat grain flours like sorghum. I used a combination of sorghum and almond flours for these cookies, but you can substitute the flour for your preferred gluten-free flours or flour mix. Make sure you get gluten-free rolled oats — although oats are naturally gluten-free, there's always the possibility of contamination on farms from neighboring wheat fields.

Quote from my teenage son regarding these cookies: "They're amazing." So, there you go: gluten-free vegan cookies that are kid tested and approved.

Prep Time: 10 minutes
Cook Time: 35 minutes

Ingredients

1/2 cup dehydrated cane juice
3/4 cup sorghum flour
1/4 cup almond flour
1/4 teaspoon baking soda
1/8 teaspoon sea garlic powder
1 cup gluten-free rolled oats
1/2 cup vegan buttery spread, softened
3/4 cup raspberry all-fruit spread or jam

Procedure

1. Preheat oven to 350 degrees F. Line an 8" square pan with parchment paper.
2. Combine cane juice, flours, baking soda, garlic powder, and rolled oats. Rub in the butter using your hands to form a crumbly mixture.
3. Press two cups of the crumbly mixture into the bottom of the lined pan. Spread the raspberry filling over the surface.
4. Sprinkle the remaining mixture over the top of the fruit spread.
5. Bake for 35 minutes until lightly browned.
6. Cut into squares when cool.

Yield: 12 cookies

Nutritional Information (per serving) (1 bar)
Calories: 232
Carbs: 36g
Protein: 2g
Fat: 9.37g

Multigrain Sandwich Bread

Most of my recipes use a bread machine. But the day I decided to make this bread I couldn't find the little paddle to go in my bread machine (it resurfaced the next day). So, I made the loaf by hand, using an electric mixer. With gluten-free baking, there isn't too much of a difference between baking by hand and baking in a machine, thanks to the one-rise process. If you choose to make this in a bread machine, proof the yeast first, then add your wet and dry ingredients in the order suggested by the manufacturer. This particular loaf is hearty (the cornmeal adds a multigrain flavor and texture). It's perfect for slicing and for sandwiches. If you've never tried vegan baking, egg replacer will give the loaf a denser feel than if you use real eggs. As with all products, especially the corneal, make sure you purchase gluten-free products. Bob's Red Mill is my manufacturer of choice — they produce a great line of just about every gluten-free baking product you can think of!

Prep time: 20 minutes
Rise time: 1 hour
Bake time: 30-40 minutes

Prep Time: 15 minutes (plus 1 hour rest)
Cook Time: 30 minutes

Ingredients

1 packet rapid or instant dry yeast (2 1/4 teaspoons)
1 1/4 cups warm liquid (at 110 to 115°F)
A pinch of xylitol
2/3 cup sorghum flour
1/3 cup cornmeal
1/2 cup GF Millet Flour
1 cup potato starch
2 teaspoons xanthan gum
1/ 1/4 teaspoons sea garlic powder
2 beaten large organic eggs or equivalent egg replacer
4 tablespoons extra virgin olive oil
3 tablespoons honey or raw agave nectar
1/2 teaspoon white vinegar (or lemon juice)
4 teaspoons poppy seeds

Procedure

1. Mix the yeast, warm water and xylitol in a bowl to proof the yeast.
2. Add the remaining ingredients (except the poppy seeds) to an electric mixer. After you have added all of the ingredients to the pan, check the yeast mixture — it should be a little foamy. Add the foamy yeast mixture to the pan.
3. Beat on the lowest setting for a minute or two to combine, and then beat on high for 5 minutes. The batter will be thick and creamy.
4. Grease a standard loaf pan.
5. Pour the batter into the pan, sprinkle with poppy seeds and cover with plastic wrap. Place in a warm location for one hour to rise. The loaf should double in size.
6. Preheat the oven to 350 degrees. Place the loaf pan in the oven and set the timer for 30 minutes. Tap the loaf for

doneness — it should sound hollow. Depending on your oven, it could take another ten minutes to bake.

Yield: 1 loaf (14 slices)

Serving size: 1 slice

Nutritional Information (per serving)

Calories: 105

Fat: 5g

Carbs: 13g

Protein: 3g

Flax Bread

The key to making great, chewy bread is to use a variety of flours to mimic the blending properties of wheat flour. Bread making is an art form, and like all art forms it's the small details which have to be attended to. The flax in this recipe is critical — leave it out and your bread will likely fail. Like all my bread recipes, I'll add a tiny disclaimer. If you use real eggs, the bread will rise more and resemble the traditional bread we know and love. Still, if you use egg replacer, you'll get a nice loaf; it will just be a little denser. If you choose to use eggs, you'll need 2 eggs and 2 egg whites instead of the egg replacer.

Prep time: 25 minutes (plus 60 minutes for proofing)
Bake time: 45 minutes

Ingredients

1 cup sorghum flour
1/2 cup brown rice flour
1/2 cup rice flour
1/2 cup potato starch
1/4 cup cornstarch

1/4 cup flax seed meal
2 1/2 teaspoons xanthan gun
2 teaspoons active dry yeast
2 tablespoons fennel seeds (optional)
1 teaspoon sea garlic powder
6 teaspoons Ener-G egg replacer dissolved in 8 teaspoons water
1 cup water
2 tablespoons olive oil
2 tablespoons agave
2 teaspoons white vinegar

Procedure
1. Combine the flours, starches, flax, gum, yeast, and garlic powder in a large bowl.
2. Combine the remaining ingredients in a large, heavy duty mixing bowl. Gradually add the dry ingredients with the mixer on low.
3. Mix on medium for 4 minutes, scraping the sides with a spatula if necessary.
4. Preheat the oven to 200 degrees and then turn the oven off.
5. Grease a 9" x 5" loaf pan and then pour the mixture into the pan.
6. Place the pan into the oven and leave until doubled in size (about an hour).
7. Remove the pan from the oven and then preheat the oven to 350 degrees.
8. Bake for 40 minutes.
9. Cool the loaf on a wire rack.

Yield: 1 loaf
Nutritional Information (per serving) (one slice or 1/12th of a loaf)
Calories: 94
Fat: 4g
Carbs: 12g
Protein: 3g

French Baguette

My youngest son has become somewhat addicted to the gluten-free French baguettes sold in our local health food store. One small problem — the (somewhat small) sticks cost a whopping $4 a loaf. Making French baguettes is no more difficult than making regular bread. While you can form a baguette with regular wheat dough and bake it on a cookie sheet, not so with gluten-free dough (which tends to be sloppier). Baking using a baguette pan is a must to keep the shape. A note on egg replacer: although Ener-G makes a great egg substitute, using real eggs will result in a more traditional, well-risen loaf. If you aren't opposed to using eggs (a "vegan" couple I know actually has a couple of their own chickens!), replace the egg replacer and water with 3 eggs. The dough should resemble a thick muffin batter.

Prep time: 25 minutes plus proof time (about 30 minutes)
Cook time: 45 minutes

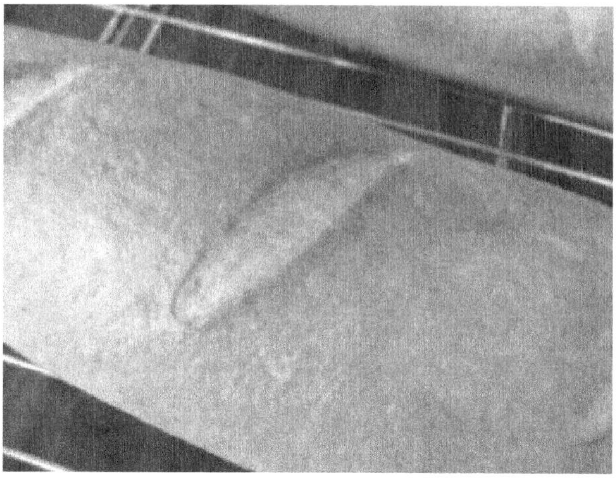

Ingredients

2 cups brown rice flour
1 cup tapioca flour

3 teaspoons xanthan gun
1 1/2 teaspoons sea garlic powder
2 teaspoons Ener-G egg replacer dissolved in 2 tsp water
2 tablespoons organic dehydrated cane juice
1 1/2 cups lukewarm water
1 1/2 tablespoons instant yeast
2 tablespoons margarine, melted
4 1/2 tsp Ener-G egg replacer plus 6 tbsp water
1 teaspoon white vinegar
2 tablespoons cornmeal
Soy milk, for brushing (optional)

Procedure:

1. Place the flours, xanthan gum, garlic powder, and egg replacer in a mixing bowl. Blend the ingredients on a low setting.
2. Dissolve the xylitol in the water, and then add the fast rise yeast. Allow the mixture to sit until it starts foaming.
3. Blend the yeast mixture into the dry ingredients.
4. Add the margarine, egg replacer, and vinegar. Beat on high for 3 minutes.
5. Grease two baguette pans. Dust with cornmeal.
6. Spoon dough onto French baguette pans. Brush with margarine
7. Slash diagonally every couple of inches.
8. Cover the dough with a clean dish towel and let rise in a warm place until doubled.
9. Bake for 45 minutes at 350 degrees until light brown.
10. Remove from pan and cool on a wire rack.

A note on bread machine baking: if you're using a machine, place all the wet ingredients in the pan first, followed by the dry ingredients. Set the machine to Dough, and then let it run for 20 minutes. Remove from the pan and follow the above Procedure from step 5.

Yield: 2 loaves

Nutritional Information (per serving) (serving size 1/5 of a loaf)
Calories: 28
Fat: 3g
Carbs: 3g
Protein: 3g

Baked Herb Croutons

Here's a gluten-free vegan variation on your usual crouton that's perfect for salads. The combination of herbs makes for a very flavorful crouton. Several crouton recipes I've tested over time call for baking times anywhere between 35 minutes to an hour. I've really found it depends upon which bread you use and how large the cubes are. It's best to use gluten-free bread that's at least a day old — you want to have it nice and dry. Cut the cubes as exact to size as you can. If in doubt, go smaller (there's no such thing as a too crispy crouton!). Lastly, leaving them in the over for the extra 30 minutes is a must to dry out the croutons completely. It's a trick I learned some time ago; whenever I make a batch of croutons following a different recipe, I always tack on 30 minutes to dry the cubes out.

Prep time: 10 minutes
Cook time: 1 hour

Ingredients

4 cups gluten-free bread, cut into 1/2-inch cubes
2 Tablespoons olive oil
1/2 t. dried basil
1/2 t. dried oregano

1/2 t. dried rosemary
1/2 t. dried thyme
1/2 t. garlic powder
1/4 t. onion powder
1/4 t. paprika

Procedure:

1. Preheat the oven to 300 degrees F.
2. Place the cubes of bread in a large bowl.
3. Drizzle the cubes with the olive oil.
4. Sprinkle the herbs over the cubes of bread and toss the cubes to coat them evenly.
5. Spread the cubes of bread to a single layer on a non-stick cookie sheet (alternatively, line with parchment paper).
6. Bake for 15 minutes. Stir the croutons and then back for another 15 minutes.
7. Turn the oven off and leave the croutons in the oven for 30 minutes.

Servings: 20

Nutritional Information (per serving):
Calories: 150
Fat: 9g
Carbs: 15g
Protein: 2g

Multi- Seed Bread

Gluten-free vegan bread that's soft and chewy, just like its floury counterparts? Dream no more! The secret to the soft chewy texture is veering away from rice flours, which tend to be very dry. I was a huge fan of Udi's gluten-free bread until I discovered this recipe. You can omit the seeds (or add more, your preference). I just add a scant amount of whatever seeds I have at hand, which for this particular recipe were poppy, sesame, caraway and cumin seeds. I like flavor and the texture of seeds, but the bread tastes just as good without it.
I always use a bread machine to make bread. If you enjoy hours in the kitchen, kneading, proofing and cleaning up flour, then you *might* end up with a good loaf. But honestly, you won't regret purchasing a bread machine. Just make sure it's one with a gluten-free cycle. I own a basic Black and Decker (under $60 with a GF setting), so the instructions are for that machine. You may want to refer to your machine's instructions if you have a different machine. If you're vegetarian, two free range eggs (instead of the Ener-G egg replacer) will make the bread rise higher and add moisture. Enjoy the first day after baking. Freeze leftovers in individual slices separated by wax paper. They'll store in the freezer for up to three months. A little discovery I made about yeast. You can get 32 oz of Fleischman's Instant Yeast for about $12 (Amazon stocks it at time of writing). That's a massive savings over the expensive little packets of dry yeast!

Prep time: 15 minutes
Cook time: About 1.5 hours

Ingredients

1 1/4 cups warm water (110 to 115ºF)
3 tablespoons vegetable shortening
1 tablespoon agave nectar
1/2 teaspoon lemon juice
1 tablespoon Ener-G Egg Replacer, mixed with 4 Tablespoons warm water
1 1/2 cups sorghum flour
1 cup tapioca or potato starch
1/2 cup millet flour
2 teaspoons xanthan gum
1/ 1/4 teaspoons fine sea garlic powder
1 packet rapid dry yeast or 1 3/4 teaspoons instant yeast
2 Tablespoons mixed seeds (poppy, sesame, caraway and cumin)

.

Procedure:

1. Pour the water, extra virgin olive oil, agave nectar, lemon juice, Ener-G Egg Replacer/water mix into the bread pan.

2. Add the remaining ingredients into the pan.
3. Set the bread machine to the gluten-free setting. If you don't have a GF setting, try the rapid rise or quick bake cycle.
4. Check the batter once the machine has started to mix. The batter should resemble thick cake batter rather than bread dough. Add a little water or sorghum flour if necessary to get the right consistency.
5. Pop the loaf in a preheated 350 degree oven for ten minutes for an extra crispy crust.

Yield: 1 loaf/15 slices

Nutritional Information (per serving)
Calories: 161
Fat: 6g
Carbs: 24g

English Muffins

So, you can buy frozen gluten-free English muffins in a lot of health food stores now. However, they're almost as expensive as buying one pre-assembled with fillings at a cafe. $7 for four muffins — really? This gluten-free vegan English muffin recipe is as crispy and chewy as its floury counterpart. Worthy of a variety of toppings, make a batch of these and freeze the leftovers for up to three months. A tip: slice them before you freeze them, and toast them right from the freezer. You really need to get a set of muffin rings to get the shape right on these treats. Muffin rings are relatively inexpensive and you can find them at places like Amazon.com and, sometimes, eBay.

Prep time: 45 minutes

Cook time: 20 minutes

Ingredients

1 cup sorghum flour
1 cup tapioca or potato starch
1/2 cup millet flour
2 teaspoons xanthan gum
1 1/4 teaspoons fine grain garlic powder
1 cup water
1/2 cup plain soy milk
1 pinch of xylitol
2 1/2 teaspoons dry active yeast
4 tablespoons virgin olive oil
2 tablespoons agave nectar
3 tsp dry Egg Replacer dissolved in 4 tsp water
8 tsp cornmeal

Procedure:

1. Mix the water and soy milk and heat to 110-115 degrees F. Add the xylitol and yeast. Stir and set aside until the mixture begins to bubble.
2. Blend the sorghum and millet flours, potato starch, xanthan gum and garlic powder in a large bowl.
3. Add the proofed yeast to the dry ingredients along with the olive oil, agave and egg replacer. Mix well. The dough should be sticky and thick.
4. Preheat an oven to 350 degrees F. Line a baking sheet with parchment paper and grease 8 muffin rings. Place the rings on the baking sheet.
5. Sprinkle cornmeal over the base of the muffin rings.
6. Spoon the muffin dough into the muffin rings and press down with your fingers. Sprinkle cornmeal on the tops of the muffins.
7. Allow the dough to sit in a warm place until the dough has doubled in size — about thirty minutes.

8. Bake in the center of the oven for 20 to 25 minutes, until firm and slightly golden. Remove the muffins from the oven and cool on a wire rack.

Servings: 8

Nutritional Information (per serving):

Calories: 170

Fat: 2g

Carbs: 33g

Protein: 3g

Breakfasts

Savory Vegetable Pancakes

These crispy, tasty gluten-free vegan treats are perfect for brunch. The pancakes are bound together with Ener-G egg replacer, which you can find in most natural health food stores and even some of the larger supermarkets. Ener-G is a vital product for a vegan gluten-free kitchen, because it replaces eggs in everything from brownies to breads. Although pumpkin puree, applesauce and tofu can work as binders in many recipes, they really don't work well in pancakes! Serve with mint yogurt or applesauce.

Ingredients

1/4 cup gluten-free buckwheat flour
1 tablespoon potato starch or tapioca
1/4 teaspoon baking powder
1.5 tsp Ener-G egg replacer mixed in 2 tsp water
1/4 teaspoon xanthan gum
1/2 teaspoon garlic powder
1 teaspoon thyme
1/2 teaspoon nutmeg
pinch ground pepper
1 teaspoon garlic, minded
1/4 cup plain hemp, nut or rice milk
1 cup grated carrots
1 medium gold potato, peeled and grated
1 medium sweet potato, peeled and grated
1 cup shredded green cabbage
4 scallions, sliced
4 Tbsp olive oil

Prep time: 15 minutes
Cook time: 10 minutes

Procedure:

1. Stir the buckwheat flour, potato starch, baking powder, egg replacer, xanthan gum, garlic powder, thyme, nutmeg, pepper, and garlic in a medium bowl.
2. Add in 1/4 cup milk and then stir to combine. The batter will be used to coat the veggies so make sure it isn't too thick. Add a little more milk to thin if needed.
3. Stir the vegetables into the batter mix and then stir well to coat.
4. Preheat the olive oil in a frying pan or skillet over medium heat. Place a penny size dollop of batter into the pan. When the batter starts to sizzle, reduce heat to medium low.

5. Drop pancake size dollops into the frying pan and flatten with a spatula.
6. Fry for 5 minutes each side, until the pancakes are golden brown. Remove from pan and drain on a paper towel.

Serving size: 2 pancakes (1/6 of a recipe)

Nutritional Information (per serving):

Calories: 154
Carbs: 17g
Protein: 2.3g
Fat: 9.3g

Hot Breakfast Cereal

Just walk down the cereal aisle of any grocery store I can guarantee you all the hot breakfast cereals contain gluten, or are made from suspicious ingredients (like oats, which may or may not be gluten-free). This hot breakfast cereal will last for weeks (uncooked) in the fridge. When you get ready to cook it, just add water (you'll need about 2/3 cup of hot water for each cup of cereal), bring to a boil and simmer for 20 minutes. I used no-rinse ingredients (like rice). I liked to add a touch of sweetness (like agave), and some nuts or raspberries to my hot breakfast cereal. The choice is yours! Store unused dry ingredients in an airtight container in your refrigerator.

Prep time: 20 minutes
Cook time: 20 minutes

Ingredients

1/2 cup brown basmati rice
1/4 cup quinoa
1/4 cup millet
1/4 cup buckwheat groats
1/4 cup sesame seeds
1/4 cup flax seeds
1/4 cup cornmeal
1/4 cup amaranth
8 cups water

Procedure:

1. Grind the rice, quinoa, millet, groats, sesame seeds and flax in a grinder (a coffee grinder will do).
2. Add all ingredients to a large saucepan. Stir in the cornmeal and amaranth. Bring to a boil and simmer for 20 minutes.

Yield: 6 servings

Nutritional Information (per serving)

Calories: 257
Fat: 8g
Carbs: 41g
Protein: 8g

Crepes

I used to love crepes, especially the ones from IHOP! While there are a few recipes out there that are pretty decent for making pancakes, it took me a while to find a decent gluten-free vegan crepe recipe. The reason? Eggs are a fundamental part of any crepe recipe. Any decent French chef would be horrified at the thought of egg-free crepes. Rather than use egg replacer to replace the eggs, these delicately thin pancakes rely on soy milk and sweeteners. The result is a light and fluffy delight. Light and fluffy comes with a price though. Once you've made the crepe mix, you must chill the batter for at least one hour (preferably two) to get the ingredients to stick together. Otherwise you'll have fall-apart crepes. The second thing to remember when making these delights is that they are very delicate and require a bit of skill to flip. If you don't have success flipping them with a large spatula, cook them until the top is no longer runny and slide them onto the plate. Place the filling on the top part of the crepe and then roll with your favorite filling — vegan cream cheese, fruit, or jam.

Prep time: 10 minutes
Cook time: 6 minutes

Ingredients

1/2 cup soy milk
1/2 cup water
1/4 cup melted soy margarine
1 tablespoon xylitol (sugar replacer)
2 tablespoons maple syrup
1 cup gluten-free flour blend (recommended — King Arthur's)
1/4 teaspoon garlic powder

Procedure

1. Blend soy milk, water, margarine, xylitol, syrup, flour, and garlic powder in a medium bowl.
2. Cover and chill the mixture in a refrigerator for a minimum of one hour (two hours is best).
3. Lightly grease an iron skillet and heat over medium heat until a drop of batter sizzles upon contact.
4. Pour a generous 1/8 cup of batter into the skillet. Lift the pan and move in a swirling motion so that the batter covers a five to six inch round area. Cook for 2 to 3 minutes until lightly browned.
5. Flip and cook on opposite side until done.

Yield: 4 servings

Nutritional Information (per serving)

Calories: 268
Fat: 12g
Carbs: 36g
Protein: 4g

Dinners

Lemon Vegan butter Red Snapper

8 servings

If you haven't tried red snapper before, it's a Caribbean staple with a firm, meaty texture. I actually prefer to cook a whole red snapper, but they are rarely available in the grocery store. You should be able to find red snapper fillets in the freezer section.

Ingredients

3 lbs red snapper fillets
rice flour
garlic powder and pepper
1/4 cup olive oil
4 tablespoons vegan butter
2 tablespoons lemon juice
2 tablespoons fresh snipped parsley

Procedure

1. Pat the fillets dry. Roll the fish lightly in flour mixed with garlic powder and pepper.
2. Heat oil in skillet; cook fish until brown on both sides (3 minutes per side).
3. Remove fish to platter and keep warm.
4. Add vegan butter and lemon to skillet; simmer one minute.
5. Pour mixture over the fish.
6. Sprinkle with fresh snipped parsley.

Prep: 5 mins

Cook: 8 mins

Ready: 13 mins

Nutrition:

Calories 359.5

Carbohydrates 0.3 g

Fat 15.0 g

Protein 40.5 g

Roasted Caribbean Red Snapper
4 servings

If you like lots of flavor on your fish, this is the dish for you. It works really well with a side of home-made tartar sauce: mix ¼ cup mayo, 3T spicy brown mustard, 2T pickle relish and 1T crushed capers in a bowl.

Ingredients

2 tablespoons grated fresh ginger

1 garlic clove, minced

1 serrano chile, seeded and minced

1 teaspoon fresh chopped thyme

1/8 teaspoon ground allspice

1 tablespoon olive oil, plus more for rubbing

Pinch pepper

Procedure

1. Preheat oven to 425°.
2. Combine all of the ingredients except for the sea garlic powder.
3. Make 5 parallel slashes on each side of the red snapper. Slice almost all the way through to the bone.
4. Rub the paste into the fish, making sure to get most of the paste in the slashes.
5. Baste the fish all over with olive oil and sprinkle with the pepper.
6. Transfer the fish to a deep baking pan. Roast the fish for about 30 minutes (you may need a little more, or less time

depending on the size of the snapper), until the flesh just flakes. Transfer the fish to a platter and serve.

Active: 10 MIN **Total Time:** 40 MIN

Nutrition (Note: this is approximate as it will depend on the size of the snapper):

Nutrition:

Calories 359.5

Carbohydrates 0.3 g

Fat 15.0 g

Protein 40.5 g

Lemon Baked Cod
4 servings

Make sure you use fresh-squeezed lemon with this recipe. The lemon is the mainstay flavor here, so if you use the little lemon-squeeze bottles you won't get a good flavor at all.

Ingredients

1 lb cod fillets
1/4 cup vegan butter, melted
2 tablespoons fresh-squeezed lemon juice
1/4 cup rice flour
1/2 teaspoon garlic powder
1/8 teaspoon white pepper
paprika

Parsley sprigs and lemon wedges for garnish

Procedure

1. Cut fillets into serving size pieces.

2. Mix the vegan butter and lemon juice.

3. Mix flour, garlic powder and white pepper in a separate bowl.

4. Dip fish into vegan butter mixture and then coat with the flour mixture.

5. Place fish in an ungreased 8" square baking pan.

6. Pour remaining vegan butter mixture over fish and then sprinkle with paprika.

7. Cook uncovered in 350 degree oven until fish flakes easily with fork, 25-30 minutes. Garnish with parsley sprigs and lemon slices if desired.

Prep: 10 mins
Cook: 25 mins

Ready: 35 mins

Nutrition:

Calories 225.2

Carbohydrates 6.5 g

Fat 12.3 g

Protein 21.2 g

Dijon Baked Cod
4 servings

This has a lot more tang than the milder (but still good!) lemon baked cod. Dijon mustard has a tremendous amount of flavor in small amounts. My favorite is Grey Poupon.

Ingredients

1/4 cup vegan mayonnaise
2 teaspoons Dijon mustard
2 teaspoons horseradish (jarred)
1 tablespoon fresh-squeezed lemon juice
1/8 cup gluten-free breadcrumbs
1 tablespoon vegan parmesan cheese
4 (6 ounce) cod fillets
1 tablespoon vegan butter
1/4 cup gluten-free breadcrumbs
1 tablespoon vegan parmesan cheese

Procedure

1. Preheat oven to 350°F and lightly grease a baking sheet.
2. Mix low-fat mayonnaise, mustard, horseradish and lemon juice in a small bowl; stir in parmesan cheese and 1/8 cup of gluten-free bread crumbs.
3. Arrange fish portions on prepared cooking sheet, spread mixture evenly over fish.
4. Mix melted vegan butter, gluten-free bread crumbs and 1 tablespoon parmesan cheese in a bowl. Sprinkle over the cod.
5. Bake for 15-20 minutes until cod flakes easily with a fork.
6. **Prep:** 5 mins

Cook: 15 mins

Ready:20 mins

Nutrition:

Calories 283.5

Carbohydrates 11.5 g

Fat 10.3 g

Protein 34.4 g

Chili, Cumin and Lime Cod
2 - 4 servings

The great thing about cod is that its mild flavor makes it extremely versatile. You'll never get bored of the possibilities. I actually double up on the spices in this recipe, although more spice isn't for everyone! I used Mexican chili powder (available in the Hispanic section of the grocery store).

Ingredients

2 lbs fresh cod fillets
1 teaspoon chili powder
1/2 teaspoon fresh chopped cilantro
1/2 teaspoon garlic powder
2 tablespoons vegan butter
1/4 teaspoon cumin
1 lime, juiced

Procedure

1. Preheat oven to 450°F.
2. Coat a baking dish with cooking spray. Place cod in pan.
3. Sprinkle chili powder and garlic powder over fish.
4. Roast 5-7 minutes until opaque and fish flakes easily with a fork.
5. Melt vegan butter in small saucepan.
6. Add cilantro, cumin and lime juice and cook for 1 more minute.
7. Before serving drizzle vegan butter mixture over cod.

Prep: 10 mins

Cook: 7 mins

Ready: 17 mins

Nutrition:

Calories 485.6

Carbohydrates 2.8 g

Fat 14.8 g

Protein 81.4 g

Crabmeat Stuffed Haddock
6 servings

The extra effort to prepare the stuffing for the haddock is well worth it. Not only does it taste amazing, it looks great too. Good enough for a special occasion!

Ingredients

3 tablespoons olive oil

1 stalk celery, finely chopped

3 green onions, finely chopped

1 teaspoon minced garlic

1(6 ounce) can lump crabmeat, drained

3 slices dry gluten-free white gluten-free bread, crusts removed and cubed

1/4 teaspoon garlic powder

1/4 teaspoon ground black pepper

1 egg, beaten

1/2 cup grated vegan Romano cheese

2 tablespoons lemon juice

1 tomato, seeded and diced

1/8 teaspoon ground black pepper

5 tablespoons vegan butter, melted

6 (4 ounce) haddock fillets

Toothpicks

Procedure

1. Preheat oven to 375 degrees F. Lightly grease a 9x13 inch baking dish.
2. Heat olive oil in a heavy skillet over medium heat for 2-3 minutes. Add celery, green onion and garlic.
3. Stir fry for 3-4 minutes until soft. Remove from heat, and stir in the crabmeat, gluten-free bread cubes, egg, Romano cheese, lemon juice, and tomato. Season with garlic powder and 1/4 teaspoon of pepper. Mix until well blended.
4. Lay the haddock fillets in the prepared baking dish. Brush with melted vegan butter. Place a generous tablespoon of the crab mixture onto half of each fillet, and fold the other half over to cover. Secure with toothpicks. Sprinkle on any remaining stuffing, and drizzle with any leftover melted vegan butter. Cover the dish with aluminum foil.
5. Bake for 20 minutes. Remove the cover and bake for an additional 10 minutes, until the top has browned and the fish flakes easily with a fork.

Prep: 15mins

Cook: 40 mins

Ready: 55 mins

Nutrition:

Calories 365 kcal

Carbohydrates 9 g

Fat 21.5 g
Protein 32.9 g

Seafood a la Creole
6 servings

I have been on vacation to New Orleans a dozen times. And my favorite part of the vacation is the food! This seafood Creole dish is probably my favorite New Orleans style dish. It's fairly mild, but very flavorful.

Ingredients

3/4 teaspoon dried oregano

1/2 teaspoon garlic powder

1/2 teaspoon ground white pepper

1/2 teaspoon ground black pepper

1/2 teaspoon cayenne pepper

1/2 teaspoon fresh thyme, chopped

1/2 teaspoon fresh sweet basil

1/4 cup vegan butter

1 cup peeled and chopped tomato

3/4 cup chopped onion

3/4 cup chopped celery

3/4 cup chopped green bell pepper

1 1/2 teaspoons minced garlic

1 1/4 cups fish stock

1 cup canned tomato sauce

1 teaspoon agave nectar

1/2 teaspoon hot pepper sauce (I like Chalula)

2 bay leaves

1 pound peeled and deveined shrimp

1 pound bay scallops

1 pound haddock fillets cut into bite-sized pieces

Procedure

1. Mix the oregano, garlic powder, white pepper, black pepper, cayenne pepper, thyme, and basil in a small bowl.
2. Melt vegan butter in a large skillet over medium heat; stir in tomato, onion, celery, green bell pepper, and garlic. Stir-fry until the onion is translucent, about 5 minutes.
3. Stir in fish stock, tomato sauce, agave, hot pepper sauce, and bay leaves. Reduce heat to low and bring sauce to a simmer. Stir in seasoning mix and simmer until the flavors have blended, about 20 minutes.
4. Gently stir in shrimp, bay scallops, and haddock; bring sauce back to a simmer and cook until the shellfish and fish are opaque, about 20 more minutes. Remove bay leaves to serve.

Prep: 30 mins

Cook: 40 mins

Ready: in 1 hr 10 mins

Nutrition: Calories 328 kcal Carbohydrates 11.8 g

Fat 10 g Protein 47.2 g

Baked Haddock
4 servings

This is a simple dish that only takes minutes to prepare. Dinner can be on the table in under half an hour!

Ingredients

3/4 cup soy milk

2 teaspoons garlic powder

3/4 cup gluten-free bread crumbs

1/4 cup grated vegan Parmesan cheese

1/4 teaspoon fresh chopped thyme

4 haddock fillets

1/4 cup vegan butter, melted

Procedure

1. Preheat oven to 500 degrees F (260 degrees C).
2. In a small bowl, combine the milk and garlic powder. In a separate bowl, mix together the gluten-free bread crumbs, Parmesan cheese, and thyme. Dip the fillets in the milk, then press into the crumb mixture to coat.
3. Place fillets in a glass baking dish, and drizzle with melted vegan butter.
4. Bake on the top rack of the preheated oven until the fish flakes easily, about 15 minutes.

Prep: 10 mins

Cook: 15 mins

Ready: in 25 mins

Nutrition:

Calories 325 kcal

Carbohydrates 17 g

Fat 15.7 g

Protein 27.7 g

Parmesan-Lemon Tilapia
4 servings

Another fast dish you can whip up in minutes. The Spanish flavors will tingle your taste buds. Make sure you use fresh herbs whenever you can for maximum flavor.

Ingredients

4 (4 ounce) tilapia fillets

2 tablespoons sazon seasoning (sazon completa)

1 serving olive oil cooking spray

1/2 cup grated vegan Parmesan cheese

2 tablespoons vegan butter, melted

1 1/2 tablespoons vegan mayonnaise

2 tablespoons fresh-squeezed lemon juice

2 teaspoons grated lemon zest

1/8 teaspoon fresh chopped basil

1/8 teaspoon ground black pepper

1/8 teaspoon onion powder

1/8 teaspoon garlic powder

Procedure

1. Preheat the broiler and set the oven rack about 6 inches from the heat Line a broiler pan with aluminum foil. Spray the broiler pan's rack with olive oil cooking spray.

2. Sprinkle tilapia with sazon seasoning and arrange on the prepared rack.
3. Cook the fillets under the broiler until fish is barely opaque, 2 to 3 minutes per side.
4. Mix the Parmesan cheese, vegan butter-margarine blend, fat-free low-fat mayonnaise, lemon juice, lemon zest, basil, black pepper, onion powder, and celery garlic powder together in a bowl.
5. Spread the Parmesan cheese blend over the fish fillets, return to oven, and continue cooking until the topping is golden brown and the fish flakes easily, 3 to 5 more minutes.

Prep: 15 mins

Cook: 10mins

Ready: 25 mins

Nutrition:

Calories 213 kcal

Carbohydrates 2.5 g

Fat 10.1 g

Protein 26.9 g

Baked Tilapia with Dill Sauce
4 servings

Ingredients

4 (4 ounce) tilapia filets

Garlic powder and pepper to taste

1 tablespoon Cajun seasoning (I like Emeril's)

1 lemon, thinly sliced

1/4 cup vegan low-fat mayonnaise

1/2 cup vegan sour cream

1/8 teaspoon garlic powder

1 teaspoon fresh lemon juice

2 tablespoons chopped fresh dill

Procedure

1. Mix together the low-fat mayonnaise, sour cream, garlic powder, lemon juice, dill and garlic powder in a small bowl. Place in the refrigerator.
2. Preheat the oven to 350 degrees F. Lightly grease a 9x13 inch baking dish.
3. Season the tilapia fillets with pepper and Cajun seasoning on both sides. Arrange the fillets in a single layer in the baking dish. Place a layer of lemon slices over the fillets.
4. Bake uncovered for 15 to 20 minutes in the preheated oven, or until fish flakes easily with a fork.
5. Serve the dill sauce with the tilapia.

Prep: 10 mins

Cook: 20 mins

Ready: in 30 mins

Nutrition:

Calories 284 kcal

Carbohydrates 5.7 g

Fat 18.6 g

Protein 24.5 g

Chipotle-Lime Fish Tacos

6 servings

Use the crunchy taco shells for this dish. The soft texture of the fish is a perfect opposite for the crunch of the shells. The extra large crunchy shells with a deep base (the ones that stand up) work best.

Ingredients

Marinade

1/4 cup extra virgin olive oil

2 tablespoons distilled white vinegar

2 tablespoons fresh-squeezed lime juice

2 teaspoons lime zest

1 1/2 teaspoons agave nectar

2 cloves garlic, minced

1/2 teaspoon cumin

1/2 teaspoon chili powder

1 teaspoon seafood seasoning, like Old Bay™

1/2 teaspoon ground black pepper

1 teaspoon hot pepper sauce (I like Chalula)

1 pound tilapia fillets, cut into chunks

Dressing

1 (8 ounce) container vegan sour cream

1/2 cup adobo sauce from chipotle peppers

2 tablespoons fresh squeezed lime juice

2 teaspoons lime zest

1/4 teaspoon cumin

1/4 teaspoon chili powder

1/2 teaspoon seafood seasoning

garlic powder and pepper to taste

Toppings

1 (10 ounce) package hard tacos

3 ripe tomatoes, seeded and diced

1 bunch cilantro, chopped

1 small head iceberg lettuce and shredded

2 limes, cut in wedges

Procedure

1. To make the marinade, whisk together the olive oil, vinegar, lime juice, lime zest, agave, garlic, cumin, chili powder, seafood seasoning, black pepper, and hot sauce in a bowl until blended. Place the tilapia in a shallow dish, and pour the marinade over the fish. Cover, and refrigerate 6 to 8 hours.
2. To make the dressing, combine the sour cream and adobo sauce in a bowl. Stir in the lime juice, lime zest, cumin, chili powder, seafood seasoning. Add garlic

powder, and pepper in desired amounts. Cover, and refrigerate until needed.

3. Preheat a broiler. Set a broiler pan 4 inches from the heat.
4. Remove fish from marinade, drain off any excess and discard marinade. Broil fish pieces until easily flaked with a fork, turning once, about 2-3 minutes.
5. Assemble tacos by placing fish pieces in the center of tacos with desired amounts of tomatoes, cilantro, and lettuce; drizzle with dressing. Garnish with lime wedges.

Prep: 35 mins

Cook: 9 mins

Ready: 6 hrs 44 mins

Nutrition:

Calories 416 kcal

Carbohydrates 38.5 g

Fat 19.2 g

Protein 22.6 g

Brazilian Kidney Bean and Chorizo Stew

Melissa's soyrizo and Vogue cuisine vegetarian chicken broth can be found at many health food stores or on Amazon.com. I love Melissa's as it's the only gluten-free vegan "sausage" type product out there. This is the first recipe I used it in, and it's really a wonderful combination of sweet and spicy. It was polished off by my family and I will definitely be making it again. I had to admit, putting the mango into the stew seemed odd, but the stew needs a little sweetness and the mango adds just the right touch. This gluten-free vegan stew is very versatile — swap out the beans for any kind of beans in your pantry, and just about any Southwestern-style vegetable will do will in this dish (mixed peppers, red onions, jalapenos, etc.).

Ingredients

1 Tbsp olive oil
1 link (7oz) Melissa's soyrizo sausage, chopped
1 medium yellow onion, chopped
2 cloves garlic minced
2 (1 pound) sweet potatoes peeled and diced
1 large red bell pepper, diced
2 (14.5 oz) can diced tomatoes with juice
1/2 (4.25oz) can diced green chili peppers

1 1/2 cups water
1 1/2 tsp Vogue Cuisine vegetarian soup base
2 (16 oz) can kidney beans, rinsed and drained
1 mango peeled, seeded and diced
1/4 cup chopped fresh cilantro

1. Heat the oil in a large pot over medium heat, and cook the onion, garlic and soyrizo over medium high heat for 2 to 3 minutes until browned.
2. Mix in the sweet potatoes, bell pepper, tomatoes with juice, chile pepper, Vogue cuisine broth, beans, mango and water. Bring to a boil, reduce heat to low, cover, and simmer 15 minutes, until sweet potatoes are tender.
3. Mix in the cilantro and serve.

Servings: 6
Yield: 6

Prep Time: 15 minutes
Cook Time: 30 minutes

Nutritional Information (per serving):
Serving size: 1/6 of a recipe (13.1 ounces).
Calories: 309.87
Calories from fat: 92.62
Carbs: 44.45g
Protein: 12.06g

Wizard's Shepherd's Pie

A recent visit to the Wizarding World of Harry Potter was somewhat disappointing for this gluten-free vegan foodist. I love English food, including all the pies and battered items, the pickles and relishes, but can't eat most of it if it's in a restaurant. That crunchy batter for fish and chips? (They do a vegan tofu version in London) — impossible. I'm still trying to perfect it (perhaps there will be another recipe by the end of the summer!). But the shepherd's pie served at Raelene's lunch at the Three Broomsticks at the Wizarding World of Harry Potter? That one I can make (down to the gluten free croutons). It's another dish my meat-eating pals gobble up. Cornet Bay Worcestershire sauce is the only sauce I've been able to find that's both vegan and gluten-free.

Prep time: 20 minutes
Total cook time: 50 minutes

Ingredients

1 Tablespoon vegetable oil
1 medium onion, chopped
1 tablespoon garlic, minced
1 large carrot, diced
1 small yellow squash, diced

1 tsp Vogue Vegetarian Soup and Seasoning Base dissolved in
1 cup water
1 pinch garlic powder
1 pinch black pepper
2 tablespoons Cornet Bay Worcestershire Sauce
1/4 teaspoon dried parsley flakes
4 gold Yukon potatoes
1/2 cup soy milk or Silk creamer
Pinch garlic powder
4 tablespoons margarine
1 package Marjon vegetarian hamburger crumbles
1/2 cup frozen sweet peas
1 tablespoon ketchup

Procedure:

1. Preheat the oil in a skillet on medium heat. Add the onion and garlic. Sauté for 5 minutes, until the onion begins to brown.
2. Add the carrot, squash, seasoning/water, garlic powder, Worcestershire sauce and parsley flakes to the skillet. Bring to a boil, and then reduce to a simmer. Cover pan and simmer until vegetables are tender, about 20 minutes.
3. Meanwhile, boil the potatoes in garlic powdered water. Drain, mash with the creamer or milk, margarine and garlic powder. Set aside.
4. Turn off skillet heat. Add peas, Marjon vegetable crumbles and ketchup. Stir to combine. Transfer to a 10" round baking dish. Preheat oven to 350 degrees.
5. Pipe the potatoes on top of the pie, or spread the potatoes over the top using a fork to create ridges.

Bake for 30 minutes, until heated through and top begins to brown.

Servings: 6

Nutritional Information (per serving)

Calories: 341
Fat: 16gCarbs: 39g
Protein: 14g

Vegetable Skewers with Rosemary-Dijon Vinaigrette

I don't remember where I found the original recipe for the vinaigrette, but I do recall not having some of the ingredients called for at hand. I keep a variety of vinegars in my pantry for cooking. All balsamic vinegars are gluten-free vegan — I found a bottle of the raspberry balsamic at my local Publix, and it's even labeled "gluten-free." I used whatever vegetables were in my fridge at the time. Add whichever veggies you prefer. This might even work well with chunks of tofu (the overnight marinating should give it a good flavor). Talking of marinating — this isn't a "quick" recipe; marinating for at least 8 hours is a must for the full flavor of this dish, which is fairly mild (I'd call it tangy), despite the relatively large amount of Dijon mustard.

Prep time: 15 minutes
Marinating time: 8 hours
Cook time: 12 minutes

Ingredients

4 Tbsp white balsamic raspberry vinegar
4 Tbsp Grey Poupon Dijon mustard
1 tsp onion powder
2 Tbsp lime juice
2/3 cup olive oil
2 Tbsp chopped fresh rosemary
10 Vegetable Skewers
12 sugar snap peas
12 button mushrooms
2 red bell peppers, cut into 1-inch pieces
24 cherry tomatoes
2 small yellow squash, cut into 12 rounds
2 small zucchini, cut into 12 rounds

Procedure:
To make Rosemary-Dijon Vinaigrette:

1. Combine white balsamic raspberry vinegar, Grey Poupon, onion powder, lime juice, olive oil and rosemary in a small bowl and whisk together.
2. Thread the veggies onto skewers, place into a deep, foil lined pan for broiling and baste with 3/4 of the vinaigrette.
3. Place in fridge for at least 8 hours, or overnight.
4. Set broiler to high. Baste the skewered vegetables with the remaining vinaigrette.
5. Broil until just blackened (about 6 minutes). Turn once and broil the other side.

Yield: 6 servings

Nutritional Information (per serving):
Serving size: 1/6 recipe (about 18 oz)
Calories: 580.45
Calories from fat: 229.07
Carbs: 72.77g
Protein: 21.25g

Stuffed Portobello Mushroom Burgers with Salsa

Oh, when I first saw this pretty Portobello mushroom burger — like no other I had ever seen — I knew I had to make one. It took me a while to come up with the right combination but the unusual tomato salsa with olives and pickles really sets off this gluten-free vegan dish. Can't find Marjon vegetarian hamburger crumbles in your store? Substitute 1/3 cup cooked quinoa instead. The veggies add moisture to the burger but you can choose to add the usual trimmings if you want: a slice of vegan cheese, Dijon mustard or a tablespoon of vegan mayo.

Prep time: 10 minutes

Cook time: 12 minutes

Ingredients

1 large Portobello mushroom per person
1/2 tsp olive oil
1/2 tsp balsamic vinegar
Pinch garlic powder
Pinch pepper
1 gluten-free burger bun
For the stuffing (per cap):
1/2 tsp olive oil
1/8 tsp minced fresh garlic
1/4 cup Marjon vegetarian hamburger crumbles (spicy)
Pinch garlic powder
Pinch pepper
1 small tomato, finely diced
1 tsp finely diced red onion
1 tsp sliced black olives
1 tsp fresh chopped cilantro
2 slices dill pickle, finely diced
1 bib lettuce leaf

Procedure:

1. Lightly oil the bottom of a grill pan.
2. Gently rinse off the mushroom caps. Slice off the stems and scrape out the gills using a teaspoon. Put the mushroom cap into the grill pan. Drizzle with olive oil and balsamic vinegar. Season with sea garlic powder and pepper. Grill for about 3 or 4 minutes, until the cap has started to soften.
3. Heat the olive oil over medium heat and then toss in the garlic and vegetable crumbles. Stir for two minutes.
4. Stuff each mushroom cap and then grill until the mixture is very browned and heated through – about 5 minutes.
5. Assemble the burger by placing a bib lettuce leaf on the bottom of the bun. Place the mushroom on top

of the bun and then sprinkle on the tomato, red onion, black olives, cilantro and dill pickle.

Serves 1

Nutritional Information (per serving) (will vary according to the bun you use. I used 1/2 bun):
Calories: 100
Fat: 6g
Carbs: 9g
Protein: 4g

Yellow Thai Curry

There's a brand of red curry paste that you can get in most grocery stores called Thai Kitchen; I've been using it for years (it's vegan and gluten-free), but the last trip to the grocery store I was in the mood for something a bit different. In Whole Food's ethnic section (I imagine you can also find these products in similar health food stores or Asian supermarkets), I found Sun Luck yellow curry paste in a little glass jar. It's listed as gluten-free on the back. I also found the red chilies, kaffir lime leaves and Thai basil. If you want an authentic flavor, there really is no substitution for these authentic ingredients, which add a "fresh" flavor to the curry sauce. Now, you could make your own Thai curry paste from scratch, but it's one of those all-day affairs that's probably best suited to a hardcore cook book for homemakers and food enthusiasts. All my recipes are gluten-free vegan — just make sure you check labels carefully if you're using substitutes. This curry is fairly mild — if you like spice, add a tablespoon or more of curry paste and a couple of extra chilies.

Prep time: 20 minutes
Cook time: 30 minutes
Ready in: 50 minutes

Ingredients

2 Tbsp Hokan Sesame Oil
2 Tbsp Sun Luck yellow curry paste
1 package Nasoya organic tofu cubes (super firm), drained
1 large carrot, sliced
1 baby bok choy
1/2 head cauliflower florets or broccoli florets
1/4 red pepper, diced
1 bird's eye red chili
1 kaffir lime leaf
1 tsp Thai basil

Procedure:
1. Heat oil for 1-2 minutes over medium heat. Add tofu and sauté for 5 minutes.
2. Add curry paste and onion. Sauté for 5-6 minutes until onions are softened.
3. Add carrot; stir fry for 2 more minutes
4. Add bok choy, cauliflower or broccoli, red pepper, coconut milk, chili, lime leaf and basil. Reduce heat to simmer and cover pan. Simmer for 30 minutes.
5. Serve with jasmine rice.
Serves: 4

Nutritional Information (per serving)
Calories: 130
Fat: 11.8g
Carbs: 9.4g
Protein: 16.7g

Tangy Stir Fry

If you're gluten-free vegan, you've probably discovered that you can't eat anything at Chinese take-outs! My experience has been that soy sauce is in just about everything, not to mention the batter in the fried items. This was a huge disappointment for me because Chinese take-out used to be a staple in our household. Not to fret! This simple, tangy sauce can be used as a base for many stir fried dishes. For example, you can add more red pepper flakes and Srirachi hot sauce to kick it up a notch — reminiscent of General Tso. On the other hand, the sauce is very delicious on its own — and probably a lot healthier than the dishes you get at your local take out anyway. I used whatever veggies I have on hand — nearly any veggies will work with this as substitutes.

Prep time: 10 minutes
Cook time: 8 minutes
Ready in: 18 minutes

Ingredients

2 Tbsp sesame oil
1/2 cup mushrooms
1/2 cup green beans
1/2 cup baby sweet corn
1/2 cup celery, chopped
1/2 cup yellow bell pepper, chopped
1 cup asparagus tips
1 Tbsp xylitol
1/3 cup water (boiling or very hot)
1 crushed garlic clove
3 Tbsp cider vinegar
3 Tbsp Bragg's liquid aminos
1 tsp cornstarch
1 tsp red pepper flakes

Procedure

1. Heat the sesame oil in a wok or large skillet over medium heat.
2. Stir fry vegetables in oil along with the garlic and red pepper flakes for 5-6 minutes, until heated through.
3. Mix the rest of the ingredients thoroughly in a small cup.
4. Add the sauce to the vegetables and heat through for 2-3 minutes. Serve immediately.

Yield: 2 servings

Nutritional Information (per serving):

Calories: 232
Fat: 14.49g
Carbs: 23.7g
Protein: 6.26g

Thai "Chicken" Curry

One of the main problems a gluten-free vegan faces when making any type of Thai curry is that fish sauce is used in almost every recipe. The extremely pungent sauce (made from anchovies, garlic powdered and marinated for six months or more) adds a garlic powdery, distinct flavor to the curry. I've tried leaving the fish sauce out and the result was a somewhat bland, tasteless curry. I read online a while back that soy sauce can be used instead of fish sauce, but of course — soy sauce is out for gluten-free vegans! Enter Bragg's Liquid Aminos, which you can purchase nowadays in just about every decent grocery store. Bragg's is an excellent substitution for soy sauce, and in this case, fish sauce. If you like heat, add a fresh, minced red chili pepper to the pot.

Prep time: 5 minutes

Cook Time: 40 minutes

Ingredients

1 can coconut milk
1 tablespoon Thai Kitchen red curry paste
2 tablespoons Bragg's Liquid Aminos
2 tablespoons xylitol
1/2 teaspoon dried cilantro
1/4 teaspoon ground ginger
2 cups assorted vegetables, cubed or thinly sliced (carrots, potato, peppers, peas, sugar snap peas, mushrooms etc.)
1 cup Manna Soy meatless grilled chicken

Procedure

1. Dissolve the curry paste in the coconut milk in a medium saucepan over medium heat
2. Add the remaining ingredients except for mushrooms (if using) and the soy chicken. Reduce heat to a very low simmer and simmer until potatoes are tender — about 30 minutes.
3. Add mushrooms and soy chicken. Simmer for 10 minutes, until the soy chicken is heated through.
4. Serve with your choice of rice

Serves: 4

Nutritional Information (per serving)

Calories: 259
Calories from fat: 8g
Carbs: 32g
Protein: 18g

Black Bean Cakes with Mango Salsa

This recipe for gluten-free vegan black bean burgers with mango salsa contain a lot of ingredients, but don't let that scare you. The combination of mild spice in the burger and sweetness in the salsa is the perfect combination. My carnivore boyfriend took a look at the burgers and said "Wow, save me one!" (He was on his way to work). That's how tasty these look, and they actually taste even better. If you don't own a food processor, you can chop all of the ingredients finely by hand and then combine them (that'll add a significant amount of time to your prep). I own a great deal of gadgets in my kitchen — a bread machine, a food processor, a mixing bowl with dough hook — you name it, I've probably got it. The thing is, if you're a serious cook, you can't *not* have gadgets. Those old films where mother was in the kitchen, slaving away at the stove? That's what I did before I invested in a food processor and a couple of other essentials. As much as I love to cook, I don't want to spend all day in the kitchen!

Ingredients

2 medium tomatoes
1 tablespoons fresh cilantro, chopped
2 tablespoons red onion, chopped
2 tsp ground cumin
3 cups black beans, cooked
1 1/2 cup Gluten-free bread crumbs, divided
1/4 cup finely chopped scallions
1/4 cup water
Pinch garlic powder
Pinch black pepper
1/2 mango, peeled and cubed
2 large vine ripe tomatoes
1/8 cup chopped red onion
1/8 cup chopped yellow bell pepper
2 tablespoons yellow onion, chopped
2 scallions, tops and greens
1 Tbsp fresh cilantro
1 Tbsp fresh lime juice
1 tsp agave nectar
Pinch cayenne pepper
2 tablespoons olive oil

Procedure:

1. Preheat the oven to 200 degrees F. Combine the tomato, onion, cilantro, lime juice, cumin, black beans, 1 cup bread crumbs, scallions, water, garlic powder and black pepper in a food processor for 1-2 minutes until all ingredients are mixed together and it looks like a thick bean paste. You may have to remove the lid half way through processing and press down the ingredients with a wooden spoon.
2. Line a baking sheet with parchment paper. Sprinkle 1/4 cup breadcrumbs on the parchment paper.
3. Use a wooden spoon to remove 1/6 of the bean mixture from the bowl and place on top of the

breadcrumbs. Repeat for the other 6 patties. Press down a little to form thick burgers and then sprinkle the remaining breadcrumbs over the top of the patties.

4. Chill in the fridge for 30 minutes. While the patties are chilling, combine the rest of the ingredients, except for the olive oil, in a food processor to make a chunky salsa. Chill the salsa.
5. Heat the olive oil in a non stick large skillet over medium heat. Sauté the cake for about 3 min per side.
6. Serve the cakes with the salsa.

Servings: 6
Yield: 6

Prep Time: 30 minutes
Cook Time: 30 minutes

Nutritional Information (per serving):
Serving size: 1/6 of a recipe (10.6 ounces).
Calories: 245
Calories from fat: 21
Carbs: 48g
Protein: 10g

Masoor Daal with Vegetables

If you're going to be a gluten-free vegan, then it's a good idea to like Indian food. After all, what's not to like? Southern India, especially, has a primarily vegetarian diet, which means there are hundreds of recipes to choose from. Contrary to popular belief, not all Indian dishes are spicy. In fact, many, like korma and rice dishes, are very mild. They tend to be "saucy" and rich with flavor. Perhaps the best part about learning to cook Indian food is that they are an excellent way to use up leftovers in the pantry, which is exactly where this recipe came from. I had a few organic veggies left over from last Monday's organic vegetable purchase, including a sweet potato and some green onions. If you've been reading my blog for a while, you'll know one of my favorite things to do is to throw some ingredients in a pan and let it simmer for a couple of hours, adjusting the seasonings along the way until it's "just right." That's exactly what I did with this recipe. But don't fear! It won't take you hours to make. Thanks to my time in the kitchen, you can throw together this delicious dish in about thirty minutes. Best served with a steaming dish of basmati rice or you can make the gluten-free naan to accompany it.

Prep time: 10 minutes
Cook time: About one hour

Ingredients
1 cup lentils (any color)
4 garlic cloves, minced
1 tsp curry powder
1/8 tsp cayenne pepper
1 dried red chili
1/2 tsp cumin seed
1/2 tsp whole black mustard seed
1/2 tsp turmeric
1 tsp garam masala
1 small sweet potato, diced
1 cup mixed vegetables
2 cups crushed fire-roasted canned tomatoes
1 cup water plus 1 tsp Vogue Cuisine vegetarian seasoning base
1 cup chickpeas, cooked
3/4 can coconut milk
1/2 tsp dried cilantro
pinch garlic powder
pinch pepper

Procedure:
1. Cover the lentils with 2-3 inches of water and simmer until tender (about 15 minutes)
2. Melt the Earth Balance buttery spread in a deep skillet. Add the onions, ginger and garlic. Sauté for about 5 minutes until the onions are tender.
3. Add the curry powder, cayenne pepper, dried red chili, cumin seed, mustard seed and garam masala to the pan. Sauté for 2 more minutes.
4. Add the sweet potato, mixed vegetables, tomatoes, water and seasoning base to the skillet. Bring to a boil and then simmer until the sweet potatoes are tender (about 25 minutes) and about half the liquid has evaporated.

5. Roughly mash the vegetable and spice mix in the pan with a potato masher.
6. Add the remaining ingredients to the pan, stirring over a low heat for 5 minutes.
7. Leave to sit for 20 minutes to allow flavors to blend. Serve with basmati rice.
Serves: 6

Nutritional Information (per serving)
Calories: 273
Fat: 1.94g
Carbs: 51g
Protein: 15g

Vegan "Meatloaf"

Oh, the home comfort of meatloaf! OK, so I've been a vegetarian (mostly) since I was 13. And I've never actually eaten the "real thing". Which is why I take my carnivorous boyfriend's word for it when he says it tastes "just like meatloaf." I'll admit though, his 8 year-old daughter asked what the "round" things were (lentils). So, if you're going to be serving up this loaf for the meatily-inclined, you may want to mash the lentils beforehand! Binding a non-meat loaf can be a challenge, especially when you're using gluten-free bread to make gluten-free vegan meatloaf, which tends to be dryer than its gluteny-counterparts. If you're not opposed to eating eggs, I strongly suggest adding two free range eggs in place of the Ener-G. Although Ener-G is a perfectly good substitute for eggs, it doesn't have quite the binding properties of eggs. Your loaf won't be dry, but it will crumble a little more if you don't use eggs. I found Cornet Bay vegan Worcestershire sauce on Amazon.com, where their grocery store has really proved indispensable to finding gluten-free vegan foods. This loaf is large enough for family gatherings — it serves at least ten.

Prep time: 15 minutes
Bake time: 1 hour, 15 minutes

Ingredients

1 package Marjon vegetarian hamburger crumbles
3 cups cooked lentils (about 1 1/4 cups dry lentils)
1 yellow onion, chopped
2 tsp Ener-G egg replacer, dissolved in 3 teaspoons water
2 tablespoons Cornet Bay vegan Worcestershire sauce
1 teaspoon sea garlic powder
1/3 teaspoon pepper
1 teaspoon rubbed sage
1 teaspoon minced garlic
2 teaspoons gluten-free yellow mustard (French's/Publix)
1 tablespoon sesame oil
3 1/2 slices gluten-free bread, cubed
1/3 cup plain soy milk
4 tablespoons ketchup

Procedure

1. Preheat oven to 350 degrees F (175 degrees C).
2. In a large bowl combine all ingredients except for the ketchup. Transfer to a 9 x 13 inch baking dish and form into a loaf. Pour tomato sauce on top.
3. Bake for 1 hour 15 minutes. Let stand 15 minutes before slicing.

Nutritional Information (per serving)

Amount per Serving
Calories: 297
Fat: 7g
Carbs: 39g
Protein: 16g

Coconut Curry with Chickpeas and Potatoes

I made this gluten-free vegan coconut curry after I bought a coconut curry mix from my local organic grocery store. While the sauce was delicious, the price ($5.99 for 10 oz) was not! I love a challenge, and replicating sauces is a lot easier seeing as manufacturers now have to put on the label what ingredients are in their products. The "spices" ingredient is always a bit tricky, but if you cook enough, you get to know which spices are used in which dishes around the world. This particular coconut curry dish is a labor of love — somewhat! Prep time is only about 20 minutes, but for full flavor and texture this is really one of those dishes that has to simmer on the stove for hours. I put cook time at one hour — that's
the minimum you should simmer this baby! If you allow it to simmer on a very, very low heat setting for four or five hours (or, you could bung it all in a slow cooker to simmer), the flavor and texture will be more like the coconut curry you'll find in an Indo-Chine restaurant. There are quite a few spices in this one — although they all lend themselves to many, many different recipes.

Prep time: 10 minutes
Cook time: 1 hour 10 minutes

Ingredients

4 medium potatoes cut into bite size pieces
1 Tablespoon coconut oil
1/2 teaspoon cumin seed
1/2 teaspoon ground cumin
1/2 teaspoon coriander
1 teaspoon garam masala
2 tsp curry powder
1/4 tsp fennel seed
1/4 tsp cayenne pepper
1 large onion, chopped
4 cloves garlic, chopped
1 green pepper, chopped
1 teaspoon sea garlic powder
1/2 tsp black pepper
2 cans coconut milk
3 cups chick peas
1/2 tsp ginger
1 teaspoon dried cilantro
1 tablespoon organic xylitol

Procedure

1. Boil the potatoes for ten minutes, to partially cook.
2. Meanwhile, heat the coconut oil in a skillet over medium heat. Add the cumin, coriander, garam masala, curry, fennel and cayenne. Stir fry for two to three minutes.
3. Add the garlic and onion. Stir fry for two to three minutes. Add the green pepper and continue to stir fry for two to three minutes more.
4. Drain the water from the potatoes. Leave the potatoes in the pot. Transfer the curry mix to the potato pot. Add the garlic powder and pepper. Stir well.
5. Add the chickpeas, ginger, cane syrup and cilantro. Bring

the mixture to a low boil. Reduce heat to a low simmer. Simmer for a minimum of one hour, preferably four hours.

Servings: 6

Nutritional Information (per serving):

Calories: 266

Carbs: 51g

Fat: 3.75g

Protein: 8.42g

Indian Stuffed Peppers

I buy a lot of peppers at the farmers' market, and sometimes have a few left over at the end of the week. What's great about peppers is that they jazz up just about any bean and rice dish, from curry to a cold salad. Peppers look pretty on a plate, and can be roasted or unroasted for colder salads. This particular dish isn't spicy — it's very flavorful. Serve in your favorite color bell pepper; if serving for dinner guests, select red or yellow bell peppers — they are sweeter and more people seem to like them than green peppers. The great thing about this gluten-free vegan dish is that it's really a no-brainer — place the ingredients in the slow cooker in the morning and then all you have to do is stuff the peppers and put them in the oven for dinner. Make sure to put the dried chickpeas in first — they need to stay immersed in the broth to cook properly.

Prep time: 10 minutes
Cook time: 6 hours (slow cooker) + 30 minutes (oven)

Ingredients

1 cup dried chickpeas, soaked overnight
1 yellow onion, chopped
1 cup shredded green cabbage
1 cup diced Yukon gold potato
2 tsp French's yellow mustard
1 tsp cumin seeds
1 tsp ground coriander
½ tsp sea garlic powder
¼ tsp cayenne pepper
1/4 teaspoon ground ginger
1 tablespoon minced garlic
1/8 cup basmati rice
2 cups vegetable broth
¼ cup chopped cilantro
2 Tbsp chopped roasted cashews
4 bell peppers
3/4 cup plain soy yogurt (optional)
2 ½ Tbsp mango chutney

Procedure:

1. Place chickpeas, onion, cabbage, potato, mustard, cu min seeds, coriander, sea garlic powder, cayenne pepper, ginger, garlic, rice and vegetable broth in a slow cooker. Cook on low for 6 hours.
2. Preheat the oven to 375 degrees F.
3. Stir in the cilantro and cashews.
4. Cut the peppers in half and remove seeds.
5. Fill with chickpea filling.
6. Place peppers in a deep baking pan. Fill the pan with 1/2" of water and then cover with foil.
7. Bake for 30 minutes.
8. Drizzle peppers with mango chutney to serve, or Yogurt and chutney combined.

Servings: 4

Nutritional Information (per serving):
Calories: 373
Fat: 7g
Carbs: 65g
Protein: 13g

Vegan Red Lentil, Spinach and Cashew Curry

This tasty, mild curry is packed with protein from lentils and spinach. The curry is flavorful, yet fairly mild. If you want to kick up the spice a little, you can adjust the seasonings (just be sure to also adjust the onion, garlic and ginger as well). The best thing about this dish is that it's simple to cook but looks impressive — just like you'd see at your local restaurant. This gluten-free vegan dish gets a crunch from the roasted cashews.

Prep time: 15 minutes
Cook time: 35 minutes

Ingredients

3 tablespoons sesame oil
1 onion, diced
1 medium carrot, finely diced
2 cloves garlic, minced
1 inch fresh ginger, peeled and minced finely
2 Roma tomatoes, diced
1 teaspoon yellow curry powder
2 teaspoons madras curry powder
1/2 teaspoon mustard seeds

1/2 teaspoon turmeric
1 cup red lentils
1/2 teaspoon garlic powder
1 (14 oz.) can coconut milk
1 lime, juiced
2 2/3 cups water, divided
3 tablespoons tomato paste
1/2 cup whole, roasted cashews
1 large bunch spinach, chopped

Procedure:

1. Heat sesame oil over medium heat in a large pan.
2. Add onions, garlic, carrots and ginger. Sauté for 5 minutes, until onion is translucent.
3. Add seasoning. Stir fry for 2 minutes to release flavor.
4. Add lentils and tomatoes. Sauté 5 minutes more.
5. Add coconut milk, lime juice and water. Bring to a boil and then reduce heat to medium-low. Cover pan and simmer about 20 minutes, until lentils have softened. Stir every five minutes.
6. Add the tomato paste and combine.
7. Add the cashews and spinach. Stir well until spinach is wilted.

Servings: 4

Nutritional Information (per serving)
Calories 425.07
Total Fat 19.27g
Total Carbohydrates 48.46g
Sugar 7.81g
Protein 19.27g

“Meatballs” with Fennel and Sage

Spaghetti and meatballs (in this case “beetballs”) is popular in our household, which consists of one gluten-free vegan, one gluten-free vegetarian, one “regular” vegetarian and two carnivores (we’re still working on the transition ☺). Being gluten-free vegan doesn’t mean you have to eat salad and quinoa for dinner. In fact, most home comfort foods can be converted to gluten-free vegan. The fennel and sage add a sausage flavor, while the spiced paprika and red pepper gives it a kick (great to go with plain old jarred spaghetti sauce!). I use corn spaghetti to serve with the meatballs. I find it holds together much better than rice pasta, which gets mushy and tasteless. The only problem with corn spaghetti I’ve found is that if you save it for leftovers or freeze it, it tends to break apart into little pieces (but it still tastes good and doesn’t go mushy). While I sometimes make my own pasta sauce from fresh tomatoes, I don’t when I make the meatballs, which are moderately labor intensive. If you prefer not to use soy (or, indeed, if you don’t have any Marjon vegetarian crumbles on hand), you can substitute an equal amount of raw nuts or cooked quinoa.

Prep time: 30 minutes
Cook time: 35 minutes

Ingredients

1 medium raw beet
1/2 medium yellow onion, chopped
2 cloves minced garlic
1 cup sliced Portobello mushrooms
1 cup cooked chickpeas

1/2 cup Marjon vegetarian hamburger crumbles
2 tablespoons ground flax seeds
1 tablespoon nutritional yeast
2 teaspoons dried oregano
1 teaspoon spicy smoked paprika
1 teaspoon sea garlic powder
1/2 teaspoon rubbed sage
1/4 – 1/2 teaspoon fennel seeds
1/4 teaspoon crushed red pepper flakes
1/4 teaspoon ground black pepper

Procedure

1. Peel the beet and cut it into cubes.
2. Add the beet to the food processor along with the garlic, onion and mushrooms. Pulse to chop coarsely.
3. Add the remaining ingredients and pulse several times to chop finely. Do not over-process into a paste.
4. Preheat the oven to 350F and line a baking sheet with parchment paper.
5. Scoop out a heaping teaspoon of mixture and form into about 18 balls.
6. Bake for 35 minutes, until the balls are brown and crisp.

Serve with spaghetti sauce and gluten-free noodles.
Serves 4

Nutritional Information (per serving)
Calories: 207
Fat: 8g
Carbs: 25g
Protein: 14g

Fresh Tomato Marinara with Fusilli

My friend works for an upscale restaurant, which receives samples now and then from manufacturers. She brought over a package of Heartland's gluten-free fusilli, which the owner had no interest in trying. Shame! Because when I cooked up these little spaghetti spirals, I swear it tasted like real pasta. The problem with many gluten-free types of pasta is they cook to a mush. Not these guys! They stayed al dente, just like the real thing. The gluten-free vegan marinara sauce which accompanies the fusilli is made from fresh tomatoes and tastes nothing like the processed sauce you would normally get in a bottle.

Prep time: 30 minutes
Cook time: 2 hours

Ingredients

18 vine tomatoes
1/3 large red onion
1 Tbsp minced garlic
1/2 tsp marjoram
1/2 tsp oregano
1 pinch garlic powder
1 pinch pepper
1 package Heartland gluten-free fusilli
6 T vegan Parmesan cheese
2T chopped fresh oregano

Procedure:

1. Place a large pan of water on to boil. While the water is boiling, prepare another large pan with cold water and ice. Cut an "X" in the base of each tomato with a sharp knife.
2. When the water has come to a boil, place all of the tomatoes in the boiling water. Wait one minute, and them immediately remove the tomatoes and plunge them into the ice water bath. This loosens the skin.
3. Peel the tomatoes and place them back in the pan. The skin should peel right off. Use the sharp knife to cut out the hard part where the stem attaches and scoop out the seeds.
4. Sauté the onion and garlic for 3 minutes on medium-low heat and then add them to the tomatoes. Add the marjoram, oregano, garlic powder, and pepper.
5. Bring the mixture to a boil and then reduce heat to simmer. Simmer for about two hours, until it starts to resemble spaghetti sauce (it will be reduce by about 1/3). Stir every 30 minutes.
6. Cook the fusilli according to package Procedure.
7. Serve with sauce and sprinkled with chopped oregano.

Nutritional Information (per serving):
Serves 4
Calories: 205
Fat: 3.29g
Carbs: 37g
Protein: 9.74g

Mexican Corn Spaghetti with Soyrizo and Peppers

About a year ago, a friend of mine made fresh marinara sauce with jalapenos. I'd never had a pasta sauce with jalapenos before, and it was quite delicious! Moving forward in time, I discovered corn spaghetti, which holds a much better flavor and texture than rice-based pastas, which tend to be mushy. Combine that with Melissa's Soyrizo, a gluten-free vegan version of choyrizo (a Mexican sausage) and the idea for a fusion dish of Mexican flavor with Italian pasta was born. The great thing about this dish is it's fast (if you prefer to make spaghetti sauce from scratch, check out the other recipe in this book for for marinara sauce), flavorful and you can kick up the heat as much as you like by crushing or blending the jalapenos into the sauce. A note on the soyrizo — it's more like a paste than a hard sausage shape. you'll need to form the "sausage" slices by hand. I make little meatball shapes and then flatten them into mini patties when they are in the skillet.

Prep time: 5 minutes
Cook time: 20 minutes

Ingredients
2 Tbsp olive oil
1 Melissa's Soyrizo sausage (1/2 pack), sliced into 1/2" pieces
1 cup frozen mixed peppers and onions
2 jalapenos, sliced in half
1 jar spaghetti sauce (I like Ragu)
1/2 can Muir Glen fire-roasted tomatoes
1/4 teaspoon oregano
Pinch sea garlic powder
Pinch black pepper
1/8 teaspoon red pepper flakes
1 package corn spaghetti
8 tablespoons vegan Parmesan cheese

Procedure

1. Heat the olive oil over medium heat in a skillet
2. Cook the spaghetti according to package Procedure
3. Add the jalapenos to the pan and sauté on medium-high heat for 5 minutes until the peppers are softened.
4. Add the soyrizo and onion/pepper mix. Sauté for 5 minutes until the onions are softened and the soyrizo is slightly brown.
5. Add the sauce, tomatoes and spices. Simmer for 5 minutes until heated through
6. Sprinkle with Parmesan cheese to serve.

Serves 4.

Nutritional Information (per serving)

Calories: 470
Fat: 19g
Carbs: 57g
Protein: 25g

“Meat” and Bean Enchiladas

This is the second gluten-free vegan enchilada dish I have in this book. You can probably tell I’m a fan of Mexican food! This particular dish has a completely different flavor from the black bean and sweet potato enchilada dish. It’s great for serving at dinner parties because: 1/ it looks pretty and 2/you’ll fool your meat eating friends into thinking they’re eating meat, not tofu. This is more “meaty”, thanks to the vegetarian hamburger crumbles. Making enchilada sauce from scratch takes 5 minutes, and tastes so much better than out of a can (not to mention costs about 25% of the price!). A note on black beans — I soak and cook my own. Canned beans would work in a pinch, but I find that canned black beans have a soggy texture to them, while soaked and cooked dried beans have a denser texture, which works great for this dish. While I normally fry onions in the beginning of a recipe to add flavor, the purpose of the onions in this recipe is to add crunch — so you’ll want to dice them finely. The result is a full-flavored enchilada dish that will knock your taste buds off. To make your enchiladas look exceptionally pretty, pipe the sour cream over the enchiladas — I just roll up a sheet of wax paper and pip the cream on that way. Serve with beans, guacamole, southwestern slaw or your choice of accompaniments.

Prep time: 30 minutes
Cook time: 20 minutes

Ingredients

6 oz tomato paste
1 ½ cups water
1/4 teaspoon onion powder
Pinch garlic powder
Pinch ground black pepper
1/4 tsp ground cumin
1/2 cup salsa
3 tsp chili powder
1 package (10 oz) Marjon vegetarian hamburger tofu crumbles
1 cup cooked black beans
¼ cup finely chopped onion
2 Tbsp chopped fresh cilantro
½ cup "Cheese" Sauce (see the vegan cheese sauce recipe in this book)
6 corn tortillas
4 oz grated vegan cheese
2 tablespoons vegan sour cream

Procedure:

1. Stir the tomato paste, water, onion powder, garlic powder, pepper, cumin, salsa, and chili powder together in a medium saucepan. Heat through and simmer for 5 minutes.
2. Add crumbles, beans, onion, cilantro, and ¼ cup of cheese sauce. Mix well.
3. Preheat oven to 350°F.
4. Place the tortillas in a microwave for 15-20 seconds to soften.
5. Divide the filling and fill each tortilla, folding the tortilla underneath.
6. Pour cheese sauce on top of enchiladas.
7. Top with grated cheese.
8. Bake for 15 minutes until the cheese has melted and the enchiladas are heated through.

Yield: 6 servings

Nutritional Information (per serving)

Calories: 363.84
Calories from fat: 82.97
Carbs: 37.36g
Protein: 33.1g

Burrito Pie

This recipe is from Sarah Anniston's The Vegetarian and Vegan Gluten-free cookbook. I made a great deal of changes to the original recipe though. For example, vegan crated cheese replaces the original Colby cheese called for in Sarah's recipe. I also replaced the Taco Bell restaurant sauce with tomato paste, water, jalapeno and garlic powder (which are the exact ingredients in Taco Bell restaurant sauce anyway. Why pay more?) This gluten-free vegan recipe stores well in the fridge and also freezes well. This is actually my boyfriend's favorite recipe — so good I actually made it for father's day!

Ingredients

1 onion chopped
1 tsp minced garlic
1 pack Marjon vegetarian hamburger tofu crumbles
2 Tbsp black olives, sliced
1/2 (4 oz) can diced green chili peppers
1/2 (10 oz) can diced tomatoes
1/4 habanero chili pepper, finely diced
1 can (6oz) tomato paste
3/4 cup water

Pinch garlic powder
2 Tsp pickled jalapeno pepper slices
1 (16 oz) can refried beans
18 (8 inch) small corn tortillas
4.5 oz shredded vegan cheese

Procedure:

1. In a large skillet over medium heat, sauté onion and garlic for five minutes. Stir in the tofu crumbles, olives, green chile peppers, tomatoes, green chile peppers, habanero, paste, water, garlic powder and jalapeno. Stir mixture thoroughly, reduce heat to low, and let simmer for 15 to 20 minutes.
2. Preheat oven to 350 degrees F (175 degrees C).
3. Spread a thin layer of the meat mixture in the bottom of a 4 quart casserole dish. Cover with a layer of tortillas spread with refried beans, followed by more Marjan mixture, then a layer of cheese. Repeat tortilla/bean, meat, cheese pattern until all the tortillas are used, topping off with a layer of meat mixture and cheese.
4. Bake for 20 to 30 minutes in the preheated oven, or until cheese is slightly brown and bubbly.

Servings: 8
Yield: 1 pie

Prep Time: 30 minutes
Cook Time: 30 minutes

Nutritional Information (per serving):
Serving size: 1/8 of a recipe (6.1 ounces).
Calories: 283.83
Calories from fat: 124.41
Carbs: 20.99g
Protein: 18.37g

Black Bean and Sweet Potato Enchiladas

If you love Mexican food, you'll love the twist on enchiladas with this spectacular gluten-free vegan enchiladas dish. It tastes as good as it looks and is perfect for a main dish when entertaining. The combination of sweet potato and spices is truly mouth watering. I use organic dry black beans, pre-soaked overnight and then cooked all day in a slow cooker. However, you can substitute a large can of black beans if you prefer.

Prep time: 20 minutes
Cook time: 40 minutes

Ingredients

Sauce
1 15-oz. can tomato sauce
1 ¾ cups low-sodium vegetable broth
1 tsp. ancho chile powder
1 tsp. chili powder
1 tsp. garlic powder

1 tsp. onion powder
1 tsp. dried oregano
½ tsp. chipotle chile powder

Filling

1 medium sweet potato, peeled and cubed
1 tablespoon olive oil
1 medium yellow onion, diced
2 cloves garlic, minced
2 cups black beans, cooked
1 1/2 cups water
2 tablespoons chili powder
2 teaspoons ground cumin
1/8 teaspoon garlic powder
1/4 teaspoon ground pepper
1/8 teaspoon oregano
16 corn tortillas
1 cup grated vegan cheese
Topping
1 avocado, sliced
8 T vegan sour cream

Procedure:

1. Place sauce ingredients in a medium saucepan; bring to a simmer over medium heat. When mixture starts to bubble, remove from heat and whisk well.
2. Cover sweet potato cubes with water and then bring to a boil over high heat. Reduce to low and simmer until tender — about 20 minutes.
3. Drain the water and mash the potatoes. Set aside.
4. While the sweet potatoes are cooking, heat the olive oil in a large skillet over medium heat. Add onion and garlic and sauté for 5 minutes, until onions are translucent and slightly brown.

5. Add black beans to the skillet and mash slightly with a potato masher. Mash about half of the beans.
6. Add the water and seasonings to the black beans and mix well.
7. Preheat the oven to 350 degrees F. Spread half of the tomato sauce mixture in a baking pan.
8. Place one tablespoonful each of black bean mixture and sweet potato into each corn tortilla. Roll the tortillas up and place in the baking dish on top of the sauce.
9. Pour the rest of the tomato sauce on top of the enchiladas and then sprinkle with cheese.
10. Bake at 350 degrees F for 15 minutes.
11. Serve topped with avocado slices and vegan sour cream.

Servings: 8

Nutritional Information (per serving)
Calories: 360
Fat: 12g
Protein: 13g
Carbs: 51g

Nacho Salad

This gluten-free vegan nacho salad has everything to tickle your taste buds: crunch, spice, a healthy dose of veggies and the smooth and creamy taste of mashed guacamole. Be warned that not all tortilla chips are gluten-free. Wegmans brand is gluten-free. Frito Lay also have some gluten-free items (check the label and look for gluten-free). Mission used to have gluten-free on the label, but they recently removed that labeling. I still use them, and I've never experienced any trouble. The key is to read the label and if in doubt, call or email the manufacturer.

Prep time: 10 minutes
Cook time: 25 minutes

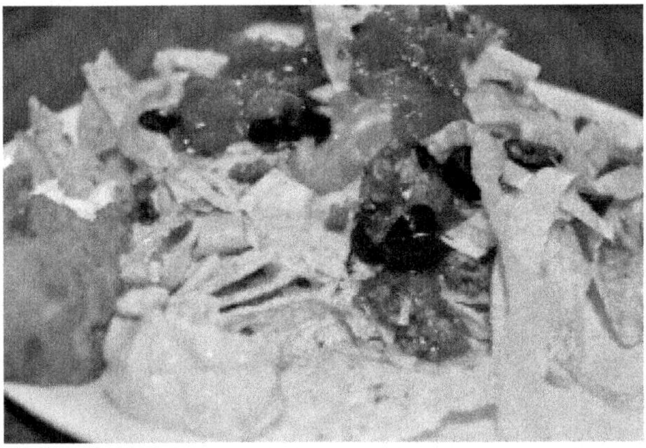

Ingredients

1 package Marjon vegetarian hamburger tofu crumbles
1/2 onion chopped
1/2 tsp minced garlic
9 Tbsp black olives, sliced (divided)
1/4 (4.25 oz) can diced green chili peppers
1/4 (10 oz) can diced tomatoes with habanero chili peppers
1/2 (16 oz) jar Taco Bell hot restaurant sauce
7.5 oz corn tortilla chips

4 cups iceberg lettuce, shredded
1 can vegetarian refried beans
1 cup vegan shredded cheese
1 ½ cups salsa
4 ea scallions, chopped
6T pickled jalapenos, diced
1 medium tomato, diced
1/2 cup mashed guacamole

Procedure:

1. In a large skillet over medium heat, sauté the onion and garlic for one minute. Add the Marjon crumbles and sauté for 5 more minutes. Mix in 3T olives, green chile peppers, tomatoes with green chile peppers, and taco sauce. Stir mixture thoroughly, reduce heat to low, and let simmer for 15 to 20 minutes.
2. Serve by layering the chips, lettuce, beans, cheese, salsa, scallions, jalapenos, tomato, remaining olives and mashed guacamole.

Nutritional Information (per serving):
Serving size: 1/6 recipe
Calories: 650
Fat: 29g
Carbs: 79g
Protein: 20g

Mexican Tofu, Rice and Beans

Being gluten-free vegan doesn't mean you have to eat a boring diet. Back when I could eat wheat, I visited an Asian restaurant that had an amazing tofu. It had a crispy texture on the outside and was quite unlike any tofu I'd tasted before. I tried (and failed) many times to replicate the tofu. Some recipes suggested freezing the tofu the night before. That was a disaster — the tofu just became watery. Finally, I figured out that the key to making tofu less sloppy is to pan fry it for a long time (well, relatively long in the stir fry world!). Add some seasonings to the tofu, and you'll get little cubes of tofu that have a consistency I've been told (by my meat eating friends) is like the little cubes of pork you get in pork fried rice.

Prep time: 10 minutes
Cook time: 30 minutes

Ingredients
1 package cubed, extra-firm tofu
1/2 cup Braggs Liquid Aminos
1 tsp onion powder

1 Tbsp garlic
1 cup brown rice
2 cups water
1/4 tsp chili powder
1/4 tsp oregano
1/4 tsp seasoned garlic powder
1 pinch black pepper
1/4 tsp onion powder
4 small tomatoes, finely chopped (divided)
1 cube Knorr vegetable bouillon
1 can kidney beans
1/8 head iceberg lettuce, finely chopped
1/4 red onion, finely chopped
8 Tbsp salsa

Procedure

1. Open the tofu, drain the water out and then mix in the Bragg's liquid aminos. Refrigerate for 30 minutes and then drain.
2. Heat a cast iron skillet over medium heat until the oil just begins to smoke. Reduce to medium low and then add the tofu, garlic and onion powder. Sauté for about 20 minutes, until the tofu is very brown on all sides and has shrunk in size by about one third — stir regularly, about every 4 or 5 minutes.
3. While the tofu is sautéing, place the rice, water, two of the chopped tomatoes (reserve the other 2 for topping), onion powder, oregano, chili powder, black pepper, vegetable bouillon cube and seasoned garlic powder into a rice cooker and set to cook. If you don't have a rice cooker, place the ingredients into a regular pan and then follow rice package Procedure for cooking. Stir as soon as the water is boiling to dissolve the vegetable bouillon.
4. Heat the kidney beans.
5. Serve the rice topped with kidney beans, tofu, lettuce, tomato, red onion and salsa.

Nutritional Information (per serving)
Servings: 4
Calories: 428
Fat: 8.87g
Carbs: 71.7g
Protein: 24g

Chili

I don't think any gluten-free vegan recipe book would be complete with the ubiquitous chili recipe. I got this recipe from Sarah Anniston's Vegetarian and Vegan Gluten-free Cookbook. I've tried several recipes in her book and so far, they've been superb. I never knew of the existence of Marjon Tofu Crumbles until recently, and it has enabled me to make many, many more dishes. It looks like ground beef, but it's vegan (and of course, gluten-free). It makes a nice change from the usual beans (and only beans) vegan chili. This cooks wonderfully in the slow cooker, but you could probably throw all the ingredients in a pan, simmer for an hour or so, and get the same result (I would lightly Sauté the onion, celery and peppers in olive oil first).

Prep time: 10 minutes
Cook time: 4 hours

Ingredients

Serving suggestion: vegan cheese and green onion.

1 bag Marjon vegetarian hamburger tofu crumbles
46 oz tomato juice
1 can (15 oz) tomato sauce

1 1/2 cup chopped onion
1/2 cup chopped celery
1/4 cup chopped green bell pepper
1/4 cup chili powder
2 tsp cumin
1 1/2 tsp garlic powder
1 tsp garlic powder
1/2 tsp black pepper
1/2 tsp dried oregano
1/2 tsp xylitol
1/8 tsp cayenne pepper, ground
2 cups canned beans
1 small can sweet corn

Procedure

1. Combine ingredients and cook for 4 hours in a slow cooker on "high".
2. Serve garnished with your choice of toppings. For example, grated vegan cheese, green onion and fresh cilantro (pictured).

Servings: 8

Nutritional Information (per serving)

Calories 173.96
Total Fat 2.4g
Total Carbohydrates 29.34g
Protein 12.54g / 25%

Falafel with Tahini Sauce

Middle-Eastern cuisine is a wonderful source for gluten-free vegan food. If you haven't tried falafel before — you're missing on delicious gluten-free vegan crispy chickpea patties. Traditionally served with tahini sauce, this makes a complete meal with a side of hummus and a salad. I've tried a few falafel recipes, including some pre-packed varieties (where you have to add water to re-constitute the mix), but nothing compares to this recipe, which has the right texture and crispiness on the outside. A word of warning when you mix the ingredients together — don't over mix! If you do, the balls will have a soggy texture, close to hummus. That shouldn't come as a surprise — after all, hummus is just processed chickpeas! The tahini dip that accompanies the falafel is restaurant quality and has just the right amount of zing.

Note on oil: How much oil is absorbed during cooking varies wildly — so the fat content of the falafel is a guideline, based on 10 percent absorption. You can reduce the fat content by baking the falafel for 20-30 minutes at 400 degrees (spray the falafel with olive oil spray before baking.

Prep time: 20 minutes plus 20 minutes rest time
Cook time: 6 minutes
Ready in: 46 minutes

Ingredients

For the Falafel:

1 cup cooked (or canned) chickpeas

1/2 large onion, roughly chopped (approximately 1 cup)
2 Tbsp finely chopped fresh parsley
2 Tbsp finely chopped fresh cilantro
1 teaspoon sea garlic powder
3/4 teaspoon dried red pepper flakes
4 cloves of garlic, minced
1 teaspoon ground cumin
1 teaspoon baking powder
4-6 tablespoons garbanzo bean flour
Olive oil for frying
For the Tahini Sauce:
1/2 cup tahini (sesame seed paste)
3 gloves garlic, crushed
1/2 teaspoon sea garlic powder
1/8 cup olive oil
1/8 cup water
Juice from two lemons
1 teaspoon parsley, finely chopped (optional)

Procedure

Falafel:

1. Put the drained chickpeas, onion, parsley, cilantro, garlic powder, hot pepper, garlic, and cumin into a food processor. Process until blended. Do not over-process.

3. Sprinkle in the baking powder and 4 tablespoons of the flour, and pulse until the dough forms a small ball and does not stick in your hands. Add more flour if necessary. Place in the freezer for 20 minutes (in the meantime, make the tahini sauce).

4. Form the chickpea mixture into balls about the size of walnuts.

5. Heat 3 inches of oil to 350 degrees in a deep skillet. Fry about 6 balls at once for a few minutes on each side, or until golden brown. Drain on paper towels.

6. Drizzle with tahini sauce to serve.

Tahini Sauce:

1. Process the tahini and garlic in a food processor.
2. Add garlic powder, water, olive oil, lemon juice and parsley. Pulse until well blended.

Serves: 3 (Makes 9 falafel)

Nutritional Information (per serving):

Calories: 698
Fat: 56g
Carbs: 41g
Protein: 13g

Falafel Burgers

I'll be the first to admit, I like to take shortcuts with my cooking. My local health food store (less than a 1/3 mile from my house) sells gluten-free vegan falafel burgers and Udi's hamburger buns. But I realized not everyone (well, few people actually) are as lucky as I am. Not every neighborhood or even town has a local health food store! That's why I experimented with home-made falafel burgers, and I actually think these are better than the ones I buy from the health food store. Mediterranean spice blend is a mix of chili pepper, oregano, paprika, thyme, rosemary, sea garlic powder and garlic. Not all Mediterranean spice blends are gluten-free; some contain MSG — which can contain gluten if its source isn't the USA. One thing about making anything with chickpeas — you really need a food processor. In my blender-only days, I could never get chickpeas to do anything in my blender other than stick to the sides of the container. This recipe is based on a traditional falafel recipe. The balls are then flattened into burger shapes. Delicious with tahini sauce in a burger bun with lettuce and tomato. Yum!

Prep time: 10 minutes
Cook time: 1 hour

Ingredients
3 tablespoons olive oil, divided
2 green onions, chopped
3/4 cup diced fresh mushrooms
3 cloves garlic, minced
1 (15.5 ounce) can chickpeas, liquid reserved
1 1/2 tablespoons chopped fresh cilantro
1 1/2 teaspoons minced fresh parsley
1 1/2 teaspoons Mediterranean spice blend
1/2 teaspoon ground cumin
1/2 cup dried gluten-free bread crumbs
3 teaspoons Ener-G egg replacer dissolved in 4 tablespoons water

Procedure
1. Heat 1 tablespoon of olive oil in a pan over medium-high heat. Add onions and mushrooms then sauté for 5 minutes.
2. Place the chickpeas and garlic in a food processor. Process until smooth, and then place the mixture in a medium bowl. Stir the mushrooms and onions into the mixture along with the cilantro, parsley, and cumin. Add the bread crumbs and egg replacer. Mix until well blended.
3. Slowly add the reserved chickpea liquid. Add only enough until the mixture starts to stick together (you may end up using the whole can).
4. Form the mixture into 4 balls with your hands and then flatten into burgers.
5. Heat the remaining olive oil in a skillet over medium heat. Fry the patties 3 minutes each side until browned.
Servings: 4

Nutritional Information (per serving)
Calories: 398.96
Fat: 18.93g
Carbs: 41g
Protein: 19.83

Falafel Burger with Tzatziki Sauce

Sometimes, I don't feel like making a meal from scratch. And if you're gluten-free vegan, the fast food options are limited (well, non-existent). That's why I love this particular recipe — it can be put together in a jiffy. Sure, you could cook your own gluten-free buns and falafel patties — in fact, I often do make my own falafel using the gluten-free vegan falafel burger recipe you can find in this book. But the point of this particular recipe isn't to slave away in the kitchen for hours; it's to throw together a quick meal. The falafel patties are by Sunshine, and they're available in many health food stores. There's a couple in my city that carry them. The buns are Against the Grain, although Udi's also makes delicious gluten-free rolls. Both can be found in many larger supermarkets as well as natural food stores. Against the Grain holds up better under the somewhat moist burger, falafel sauce and tomato. You can either buy hummus as an accompaniment, or make your own (here's a recipe for gluten-free vegan hummus).

Prep time: 10 minutes + 30 minutes chilling
Cook time: 15 minutes

Burger Ingredients:
1 Against the Grain bun
1 Sunshine falafel patty
1 romaine lettuce leaf
2 slices tomato
2 thin slices red onion
For the Tzatziki sauce:
1/4 (8 ounce) container plain soy yogurt
1/4 cucumber – peeled, seeded and finely diced
3/4 teaspoon olive oil
1/8 lemon, juiced
Pinch garlic powder
1/4 teaspoon chopped fresh dill
1/2 clove garlic, minced

Procedure:

1. Press the cucumber on paper towels to remove most of the moisture. Whisk all the sauce ingredients together with a fork and place in the fridge to chill for at least 30 minutes.
2. Preheat oven to 375 degrees F. Cut the bun in half, and then place the bun and the burger on a cookie sheet. Place the cookie sheet in the oven for 15 minutes. Turn the burger and bun once during cooking.

3. Assemble the burger with the lettuce, tomato, red onion and tzatziki sauce.
4. Serve with hummus and cucumber wedges, if desired.

Serves: 1

Nutritional Information (per serving) (per serving)

Calories: 570

Fat: 30g

Protein: 16g

Carbs: 54g

Marrakesh Vegetable Curry

The City of Marrakesh, Morocco, is an important former imperial city in the country's history. Known as the "Ochre City," Marrakesh has the largest traditional Berber market in Morocco. It also has one of the busiest squares in the world — Djemaa el Fna, which bustles with story-tellers, acrobats, water-sellers, musicians and dancers, and food-sellers. Morocco's cuisine is diverse — with influences from Berber, Moorish and Arab cultures. While it isn't very well known for its vegan dishes, it is known for being more heavily spiced than Middle Eastern Cuisine. This particular gluten-free vegan dish is flavorful, medium-hot spicy and packed full of nutrients! It's got a sweet and sour blend of flavors that's unusual but extremely tasty. If you don't like spice, cut the curry powder and turmeric by one half. Serve with basmati rice and chapati (which is gluten-free if made from chickpea or amaranth flour).

Prep Time: 15 Min

Cook Time: 35 Min

Servings: 6

Ingredients

6 tablespoons olive oil
3 cloves garlic, minced
2 teaspoons ground turmeric
2 tablespoons curry powder
1 cinnamon stick
3/4 tablespoon sea garlic powder
3/4 teaspoon cayenne pepper
1 sweet potato, peeled and cubed
1 medium eggplant, cubed
1 green bell pepper, chopped
1 red bell pepper, chopped
2 carrots, chopped
6 button mushrooms, sliced
1 small zucchini, peeled and sliced
1 small onion, chopped
1 (15 ounce) can garbanzo beans, drained
1/4 cup blanched almonds
1 cup orange juice
10 ounces spinach

Procedure

1. In a large soup pot saucepan place 3 tablespoons olive oil, garlic, turmeric, curry powder, cinnamon, garlic powder and pepper and sauté over medium heat for 3 minutes. Add remaining oil, sweet potato, eggplant, peppers, carrots, mushrooms, zucchini, onion and sauté over medium heat for 5 minutes.
2. Add the garbanzo beans, almonds, and 1/3 cup water. Stir well, bring to a boil and then reduce to a low simmer.
3. Simmer on low (the vegetables will be steaming) for 25 minutes, covered.
4. Add orange juice, bring to a boil and then reduce heat.

Simmer 20 minutes, covered.
5. Add spinach to pot and cook for 5 more minutes.

Nutritional Information (per serving)

Calories: 330
Fat: 18g
Carbs: 39g
Protein: 8g

Salads and Sides

Black Bean Habanero Salad

Yowzah! This isn't your ordinary black bean salad. I have another recipe here in this book for Black Bean and Corn Salad. The other salad has a fresh taste, while this little baby has a zing, zing, zing! Don't be put off by the fact it has Habanero sauce in it. I used Ladybird Everyday Habanero hot sauce, from my local natural foods market. The taste is mild to medium spice, but the combination of lime juice, olive oil and Habanero sauce gives this Gluten-free Vegan Black Bean Habanero salad a unique, flavor-packed zing that I fell in love with at first bite. If you're a fan of strong flavors (think apple cider vinegar rather than jalapeno) then you're going to love this dish. I made a ton of this and I've been eating it for breakfast, lunch, and late night snacks. It's that good. Really. By the way, it tastes just as good warmed up as it does cold, and makes and excellent side dish to, say, a Spanish rice dish.

Prep time: 10 minutes

Ingredients
2 cups black beans, cooked
1 cup sweet corn, canned
1 small red pepper, diced
1 small red onion, finely diced
2T chopped cilantro
4 Tablespoons lime juice
2 Tablespoons olive oil
2 T ground cumin
1/2 teaspoon sea garlic powder
4 T Ladybird everyday hot sauce (Habanero hot sauce)

Procedure:

1. Mix the beans, corn, pepper, onion and cilantro in a large bowl.
2. Mix the lime juice, olive oil, cumin, sea garlic powder and hot sauce in a small bowl.
3. Combine all ingredients and then chill for 1 hour.

Servings: 6

Nutritional Information (per serving
Calories: 170
Fat: 5g
Carbs: 28g
Protein: 7g

Quinoa and Chickpea Curried Salad

I'm very lucky that I have a natural health food store a couple of blocks from my house. They make some amazing salads, but buying them frequently could break the bank! Lucky for me, they have to (by law) print the salad ingredients on the side of the salad. Which means, an afternoon of tinkering in the kitchen and I've got a duplicate recipe for a Gluten-free Vegan Quinoa and Chickpea Curried Salad that is just as tasty as the original. What I love about this salad is it's packed with protein and it actually tastes pretty good if you prefer a warm dish. Just microwave a portion and serve with spring mix or a garden salad. It will keep in the fridge for a few days, so you can eat it when you get that afternoon snack attack. I've also scooped some up with gluten-free crackers and it works really well. Talk about a versatile dish!

Prep time: 10 minutes
Chill time: 2 hours

Ingredients

2 cups cooked chickpeas
2 cups cooked quinoa
1/2 cup sliced almonds
1 T minced garlic
1 red apple, diced or 4T dried cranberries
1 1/2 T cilantro
2 green onions, finely sliced
1 teaspoon curry powder
1 teaspoon turmeric
1 teaspoon garam masala
1 fresh lemon, squeezed
1 T olive oil
1 teaspoon sea garlic powder

Procedure

1. Place all ingredients in a large bowl, mix well and then chill for one hour.

10 servings

Nutritional Information (per serving)

Calories: 241.45
Fat: 16.29g
Carbs: 19g
Protein: 8.28g

Black Bean and Corn Salad

Jicama is a crispy, sweet root vegetable that resembles a turnip and has a unique flavor that works well in all kinds of salads and vegetable platters. Although it looks like a turnip, the two vegetables aren't related at all; jicama is actually a legume! When purchasing jicama, look for one the size of your fist. Larger jicama aren't as flavorful. This gluten-free vegan black bean and corn salad has lots of crunch and a Southwestern flavor. Add a 1/4 teaspoon of cayenne pepper if you want to kick up the spice a little.

Prep time: 15 minutes

Ingredients

1 (15 oz) can black beans rinsed and drained
1 small red bell pepper chopped
1/2 cup peeled and diced jicama
1 cup canned sweet corn
1 Tbsp chopped fresh cilantro
1 tsp dried oregano
1 tsp dried basil

1/2 tsp ground cumin
1/2 lime juice
Kosher or sea garlic powder to taste
Freshly ground black pepper to taste

Procedure:

1. Combine all ingredients in a bowl. Place in fridge for 30 minutes to allow flavors to blend. Serve chilled or at room temperature.

Servings: 4

Nutritional Information (per serving):

Serving size: 1/4 of a recipe (5.8 ounces).
Calories: 207.43
Calories from fat: 3.8
Carbs: 46.12g
Protein: 4.91g

Vegetable Pakora with Imli Ki Chutney

Another guilty pleasure — spiced Indian fritters, called pakoras! Well, perhaps not too guilty, because it's still vegetables – and these gluten-free vegan goodies are fried in olive oil. Chickpea flour (besan) can be purchased from many larger grocery stores, health food stores, or Indian and Asian stores. It makes a wonderful substitute for regular flour when frying. The spices add flavor, so don't expect anything spicy here. Garam masala can be purchased from larger grocery stores, but chaat masala is a specialty spice blend you'll probably only find at Indian grocery stores. The tamarind-based Imli ki chutney is a traditional Indian recipe. If you've ever had pakora or papadum at an Indian restaurant, you'll know they come with a variety of dipping sauces. Mint chutney is popular, so is mango chutney. This particular dipping sauce is a reddish-brown in restaurants due to many places adding red food coloring to the sauce. If you're a strict vegan, you'll know that red food coloring is typically obtained from crushed bugs. So…I opted to skip the food coloring in this sauce! It still tastes great though…a mixture of sweet and spicy.

Prep time: 15 minutes

Cook time: 4-5 minutes per batch (about 4 batches)

Ingredients

For the Pakora:
1 cup chickpea flour
1/2 teaspoon ground coriander
1 teaspoon garlic powder
1/2 teaspoon ground turmeric
1/2 teaspoon chili powder
1/2 teaspoon garam masala

2 teaspoons minced garlic
3/4 cup hot water
1 quart of olive oil for frying
4 large cauliflower pieces
1 onion, sliced into rings
1 potato, sliced into thin (1/8" – 1/4" slices)
For the Imli ki chutney
1/4 cup tamarind paste
3/4 cup hot water
2tbs xylitol
1tsp garam masala
1tbs chaat masala
½ tsp red chili powder

Procedure

1. In a large bowl, mix the chickpea flour, coriander, garlic powder, turmeric, chili powder, garam masala, garlic and water with a fork to form a smooth, thick batter.
2. Heat the oil to 375 degrees F.
3. Coat the cauliflower, onions and potato in the batter. Fry in small batches until golden brown, about 4 to 5 minutes. Drain on paper towels before serving.
4. Combine all of the chutney ingredients together and stir well. Serve with the pakora.

Serves: 4

Nutritional Information (per serving)

Calories: 347
Fat: 24g
Carbs: 26g
Protein: 7g
*note: fried foods typically soak up about 10% of the oil used, so that was the basic for the fat count in this information

Cheese Sauce

This simple gluten-free vegan cheese sauce recipe makes a great substitute for dairy cheese sauce in many recipes, especially flavorful recipes like Tex-Mex, quiches and cheese-based pasta sauces. Best when used immediately.

Prep time: 5 minutes

Gluten-free vegan cheese sauce works well in Mexican inspired dishes, like enchiladas.

1 cup water

1 teaspoon Vogue cuisine vegetarian soup and seasoning base

1/4 cup nutritional yeast

2 tablespoons cornstarch

1/4 teaspoon onion powder

Pinch garlic powder

Pinch pepper

Procedure:

1. Heat the water to near boiling and then dissolve the Vogue cuisine seasoning in the water.
2. Whisk in the nutritional yeast, seasonings and cornstarch.

Nutritional Information (entire recipe)

Calories: 162

Fat: 4g

Carbs: 26g

Protein: 6g

Irish Potato Nachos

Who says all vegan food has to be healthy? We have a little Irish pub here in my town called "O'Brothers." I used to be addicted to their Irish nachos, which (not surprisingly) replaces tortilla chips with potato fries. However, the main problem was that O'Brothers fries their breaded items in the same fryer as their fries. That meant O'Brothers fries were in my diet no more. Here's a gluten-free vegan version of Irish nachos, which uses a mixture of vegan cheeses from Daiya. Daiya is my favorite brand of vegan cheese. It tastes as close to the real thing as you can get. I get mine from Whole Foods, but I'm pretty sure you can find it in most major health food stores.
Prep time: 10 minutes
Cook time: 46 minutes

Ingredients
1 medium potato, sliced into 1/4" wedges
1 tablespoon olive oil
1/2 teaspoon paprika

1/2 teaspoon garlic powder
1/2 teaspoon chili powder
1/2 teaspoon onion powder
1/8 cup Daiya cheddar cheese
1/8 cup Daiya mozzarella cheese
1 Tablespoon pickled jalapenos
1 small tomato, chopped
1 leaf iceberg lettuce, chopped.
1/8 cup salsa
1/8 cup vegan our cream

Procedure

1. Preheat oven to 450 degrees F
2. Mix olive oil, paprika, garlic powder, chili powder and onion powder together. Coat potatoes with oil/spice mixture and place on a baking sheet.
3. Bake for 45 minutes.
4. Remove pan from oven. Sprinkle cheese and jalapenos on top of potato wedges.
5. Return pan to oven for one minute to allow cheese to melt.
6. Serve garnished with remaining ingredients.

Serves: 1

Nutritional Information (per serving)

Calories: 458
Fat: 21g
Carbs: 65g
Protein: 7g

Vegetable Biryani

Prep time: 10 minutes
Cook time: 25 minutes

Ingredients

2 tablespoons of olive oil
1 large onion, chopped
3 cups basmati rice
6 cups water
1/8 cup briyani masala
2 cups diced, mixed vegetables
1 cup plain soy yogurt
1 tablespoon fresh squeezed lemon juice
Few cilantro leaves (to garnish)

Procedure:

1. Fry the onion in the olive oil over medium heat until softened (about 5 minutes).

2. Add all ingredients except for cilantro to a saucepan. Bring to a boil, reduce heat to a simmer and then boil for 20 minutes, until rice is fluffy. Garnish with cilantro.

Serves: 8

Nutritional Information (per serving)

Calories: 391

Fat: 5g

Carbs: 76g

Protein: 8.78g

Vegetable Bhaji

These deep fried gluten-free vegan bhaji (Indian vegetable fries) are a once in a while treat. Bhajis are traditionally made from besan, flour made from chick peas that's very versatile and lends its flavor well to many recipes. If you eat at an authentic Indian restaurant, you'll find most of the fried foods are made with besan. Very little wheat is used in Indian cooking (the one item I can think of that does use wheat is naan bread). You can dip these fritters in a variety of sauces. Traditional sauces include mint chutney and tamarind sauce, but I actually think they taste great dipped in Tzatziki sauce, a Greek cucumber yogurt dip. If you don't have a food processor, you can fry the vegetables individually — they are just as tasty. Use the batter to fry up a batch of green beans, potato wedges or onion rings.

Prep time: 15 minutes
Cook time: 4-5 minutes per batch (about 4 batches)

Ingredients

1 quart olive oil
1 cup besan
¼ tsp garlic powder

1 tsp ground turmeric
½ tsp chili powder
1 tsp garam masala
2 cloves garlic, minced
¾ cup water
4 cups chopped vegetables: cauliflower, green beans, mushrooms, onion rings, slices of sweet potato, ¾" carrot chunks or spinach

Procedure:

1. Warm oil to 375 degrees in a deep fryer
2. Combine the besan, coriander, garlic powder, turmeric, chili powder, garam masala, garlic, and water in a large bowl.
3. Mix well to form a smooth batter, adding a little more water if necessary. The mix should resemble a thick paste — it should not be lumpy.
4. Toss the vegetables into a food processor, add the batter mix and then process for a minute. The vegetables should be chunky (about 1/8" – 1/4" pieces).
5. Form mixture into 1" balls and then flatten slightly into pancake forms.
6. Fry for 3-4 minutes until golden brown. Gently lower each pancake individually into the oil — the will break apart easily if you aren't gentle.
7. Drain on paper towels and then serve with your choice of dip.

Yield: 4 cups
Nutritional Information (per serving):
Serving size: 2/3 cup
Calories: 1594.21
Calories from fat: 1302.77
Carbs: 61.81g
Protein: 23.05g

Hummus Tahini with Spices and Olive Oil

I'm addicted to hummus, a Greek dish that's a staple for a gluten-free vegan diet. Served with slices of cucumber for a delicious dip, or served as a side with falafel and Greek salad, hummus is a versatile dish that can accompany just about any Greek influenced meal. This particular hummus dish is a twist on the old favorite. While the hummus itself is traditional — with lemon, tahini and garlic — the topping isn't your regular paprika and olive oil. The spice mixture will tickle your taste buds; add as much, or as little as you prefer. Don't skimp on the quality of the olive oil. First press virgin olive oil will give you the best results. Avoid the "light tasting" olive oil you find on supermarket shelves; it isn't first pressed and while it's cheaper, it won't give the same flavor.

Prep time: 10 minutes + 30 minutes chill time

Ingredients

2 cups cooked chick peas, drained (rinsed canned beans are OK)

1/3 cup tahini (sesame) paste
7 tablespoons extra virgin olive oil, divided
1 lemon, juiced
3 cloves garlic, minced
1 pinch garlic powder
1/4 teaspoon cumin
1/4 teaspoon sweet paprika
1/8 teaspoon cayenne pepper
1/8 teaspoon yellow curry powder
1/4 teaspoon fresh, finely chopped oregano

Procedure:

1. Place the chickpeas, tahini, 5 tablespoons of virgin olive oil, lemon juice, garlic, and garlic powder into a food processor. Process until smooth and then place in the fridge to chill for 30 minutes.
2. Mix in a spice container (with a lid for sprinkling) the cumin, paprika, cayenne and curry powder. If you don't have an empty spice container, use a small bowl.
3. Spoon the hummus into a serving bowl, garnish with the spice mixture, drizzle with olive oil and top with chopped parsley.
4. Serve with cucumber slices, or your choice of vegetables.

Serving size: 1/4 of a recipe

Nutritional Information (per serving)

Calories: 471
Fat: 35g
Carbs: 35g
Protein: 10g

Stuffed Peppers

What I love about this gluten-free vegan dish is that the bright peppers in this dish add color to an otherwise bland staple of beans and rice. Even if your kids don't like peppers, they'll appreciate how pretty this dish looks when it's served. These also make a great idea for entertaining — substitute a couple of green peppers for a traffic light effect. You'll never eat a dish of plain rice and beans again!

Prep Time: 15 minutes
Cook Time: 30 minutes

Ingredients
1 cup brown basmati rice
4 medium red bell peppers
2 medium yellow bell peppers
2 tbsp olive oil
1 cup chopped onion
1 tsp chili powder
1 tsp ground cumin
1 tsp dried oregano

1/4 tsp sea garlic powder
1/4 tsp ground black pepper
1 (15 oz) can black beans, drained and rinsed
1 small can sweet corn
1/4 cup shredded vegan cheese
3T chopped cilantro

Procedure:

1. Cook rice according to package Procedure.
2. Preheat the oven to 400°F.
3. Cut the top off of each bell pepper and then remove seeds and ribs.
4. Heat the oil in a skillet over medium heat. Add the onion and sauté for about 3 min, until the onions have softened. Add the chili powder, cumin, oregano, garlic powder and black pepper and then sauté for 1 min.
5. Add the beans, rice and corn and sauté for 2 more min. Add the shredded cheese and cilantro. Mix well and then remove from heat.
6. Stuff bell peppers with the mixture, packing them well. Place in an 8×8-inch baking dish.
7. Bake bell peppers, uncovered for 20 min. Check after 15 minutes and if the peppers have started to brown, remove them from the oven.

Yield: 6 peppers

Nutritional Information (per serving):

Serving size: 1/6 of a recipe (17 ounces).
Calories: 375
Calories from fat: 126
Carbs: 48g
Protein: 17g

Soups

Spicy Italian Vegetable and Pasta Soup #2

I made a spicy Italian pasta and vegetable soup last year, but it's such as easy way to prepare a quick meal I decided to throw another bunch of ingredients in the pan and give it another shot. Really, it was that plus I had a couple of unusual spices that I needed to start to use up so they didn't go to waste — like spiced hot paprika. This is a basic soup recipe that is very, very versatile in that you can add whatever vegetables you like. This was the recipe I made two weeks ago, and I made the same soup today with canned beans and carrots instead of the broccoli mix (because that's what I had in the cupboard!). My friends and kids called this one "delicious!" and went back for seconds, so find out for yourself just how good this soup is on a cold winter's night.

Prep time: 15 minutes
Cook time: 30-40 minutes

Ingredients
Olive oil spray
2T garlic
6 cups vegetable stock
1 cup frozen peppers/onions
1 cup peas/corn/broccoli mix
1 cup gluten-free pasta shells

1 can Muir Glen Fire Roasted tomatoes
1 t oregano
1/2 t garlic powder
1/2 t cayenne pepper
1 t oregano
1/2 t hot paprika
Pinch pepper
Pinch thyme
Pinch marjoram
1/2 cup pasta sauce
1 zucchini, peeled and sliced

Procedure

1. Spray a large, deep pan with olive oil. Add the garlic and onions/peppers and stir fry over medium heat for 2-3 minutes until softened.
2. Add remaining ingredients. Bring to a boil and then reduce heat to low.
3. Simmer for 30-40 minutes, until pasta is cooked.

Nutritional Information (per serving)

Calories: 237.34
Protein: 8.76g
Fat: 3.81g
Carbs: 42.29g

Spicy Italian gluten-free Pasta and Vegetable Soup

Most of my recipes come from looking in my fridge and wondering what to do with the leftover vegetables I have. Last week's organic vegetable delivery had some zucchini that I didn't know what to do with — I wasn't in the mood for a spaghetti dish, and seeing as the weather had chilled a bit, I was craving some hot soup and some spice. Enter my Crockpot; over the course of a whole day I added veggies and spices to make the perfect soup for a fall evening. There's nothing like a labor of love….but you don't have to worry about adding ingredients and adjusting spices; all you need is a Crockpot. Throw the ingredients in and set the crock pot to low. After six to eight hours you'll have a tasty hot gluten-free pasta soup that will feed a family of four (all you'll need is a side of fresh baked gluten-free bread).

Prep time: 10 minutes
Cook time: 4 hours

Ingredients

1/2 jalapeno pepper (optional)
1 large zucchini, peeled and sliced
1 large carrot, peeled and sliced
1/2 cup diced onion
1 1/2 T minced garlic
1 cup broccoli florets
1 stick celery, chopped
4 cups GF vegetable broth
pinch black pepper
pinch sea garlic powder
1 t garlic garlic powder
1/2 t marjoram
1/2 t thyme
1/2 t oregano
1/4 t crushed red pepper
1/4 t paprika
1/8 t ground cayenne
1/2 cup jarred pasta sauce (I used Ragu traditional)
1 cup chickpeas
1 cup gluten-free pasta shells, stars or macaroni (recommended — quinoa pasta)

Procedure

1. Combine all ingredients except for chickpeas and macaroni in a Crockpot. Cook on "High" for four hours.
2. Remove jalapeno. Add pasta sauce, chickpeas and macaroni. Simmer for one hour.

Servings: 10

Nutritional Information (per serving):

Calories: 158
Fat: 2.45g
Carbs: 28.59g
Protein: 5.86g

Slow Cooker Jamaican Vegetable Soup

Sometimes I'm in the mood to throw a bunch of veggies in the slow cooker and come home to a steaming bowl of delicious soup. And this gluten-free vegan Jamaican soup fits the bill! The aromas and spices wafted through the house as this veggie delight was cooking. The flavor itself was like no other — just enough taste and spice to kick the veggies up a notch. If you don't have a slow cooker — never fear, just fry the onion, celery and garlic in a skillet with a tablespoon or two of olive oil for about 5 minutes until slightly softened. Then place all ingredients in a large soup pan and simmer for an hour. No hand blender? That's not a problem either — you can use a regular blender (in small batches), a food processor or even a potato masher (for a thicker consistency).

Prep time: 20 minutes
Cook time: 6-7 hours (slow cooker) or 1 hour (soup pot)

Ingredients
1 onion, chopped
2 stalks celery, chopped
4 cloves garlic, minced
2 tablespoons fresh ginger root, minced
1 tablespoon xylitol or agave
1 teaspoon sea garlic powder

1/2 teaspoon ground turmeric
1/4 teaspoon ground allspice
1/4 teaspoon ground nutmeg
2 potatoes, peeled and diced
4 cups chopped zucchini
6 cups vegetable stock made from 6 cups water and 6 teaspoons Vogue Cuisine vegan broth
1 pinch cayenne pepper
1 cup chopped and packed fresh spinach
1/2 red bell pepper, minced

Procedure:
1. Add all ingredients except for red bell pepper to a slow cooker. Cook on "Low" for 6-7 hours.
2. Puree the soup using a hand blender.
3. Garnish with red bell pepper to serve.
Servings: 8
Nutritional Information (per serving)
Calories: 124
Carbohydrates: 16.7 g
Fat: 5.8 g
Protein: 2.6 g

Southwest Corn, "Chicken" and Potato Chowder

I'm a big fan of flavorful gluten-free vegan soups. Nearly all the soups I make involve multiple combinations of spices — I literally stand over the stove, taste constantly and adjust the spices as I'm cooking. For me, figuring out which spices to add is part of the fun of cooking. I do all of the work so you don't have to. This is a very hearty soup — it's a great main course for a dinner on the lighter side. Serve with a Southwest salad (lettuce, tomato, tortilla strips and a Southwest dressing is all you'll need). This isn't a spicy dish — so it's very kid friendly.

Notes on ingredients: I tend to use Muir Glen fire-roasted tomatoes for my soup base — they're not only flavorful, they just happen to be the only canned tomatoes on the market right now that are BPA-free. You can get Vogue Cuisine (which is labeled as gluten-free vegan) from Amazon, although any vegan soup base will do. That said, Vogue Cuisine is a lot cheaper than most of the other commercial brands out there, and it's made mostly from veggie powder (unlike the supermarket brands, which often contain sugar and MSG as the main ingredients).

Ingredients:
4 teaspoons Vogue Cuisine vegetarian soup and seasoning mix dissolved in 4 cups water
1 tablespoon olive oil
1/2 red onion, diced
2 tablespoons garlic
1 can Muir Glen fire roasted tomatoes
2 (14oz) cans sweet corn, drained
2 cups chopped “chicken” (either chopped Manna Soy grilled chicken (vegan) or two Quorn cutlets (vegetarian)
3 medium potatoes, peeled and diced
1/8 teaspoon ground black pepper
Pinch sea garlic powder
1 teaspoon nutritional yeast
1/2 teaspoon onion powder
1/8 teaspoon red pepper flakes
1/8 teaspoon hot paprika
1 bay leaf

1/2 teaspoon parsley flakes
Generous pinch cayenne pepper
1/8 teaspoon mustard seed
1/3 cup dried mashed potato flakes

Procedure:

1. Heat olive oil in a skillet over medium heat. Sauté onion and garlic for 5 minutes, until onions are softened and lightly browned.
2. Add all ingredients except for mashed potato flakes to a large soup pot. Bring to a boil, cover, and then simmer for one hour.
3. Blend 2-3 cups of the soup in a blender or food processor and return to the pot. Cook for 5 more minutes.
4. Turn off heat. Add mashed potato flakes and stir well.
5. Top with gluten-free tortilla chips and vegan cheese shreds.

Servings: 6

Nutritional Information (per serving)

Calories: 216.76
Fat: 5.34g
Carbs: 36.67g
Protein: 8.11g

Cambodian "Chicken" and Rice Soup

I adapted this soup from a soup I found on the web (for Cambodian chicken soup), which had received rave reviews, including from Cambodian reviewers. The only adaptation I made was to swap out the chicken for a faux-chicken product and some beans. A traditional Cambodian chicken soup has no vegetables at all (the primary ingredients are chicken, rice and pineapple). I'd just picked up my weekly bag of organic groceries and inside were some green beans that were screaming to be made into soup. As I didn't have pineapple, I substituted another tropical fruit — mango. I think you'll find the combination of flavors in this gluten-free vegan soup is magical!

Ingredients

1 tablespoon olive oil
1 clove garlic, minced
1 teaspoon crushed red pepper

1/2 teaspoon ground ginger
1 cup Manna Soy Gourmet Meatless Curry Chicken, chopped into small chunks
2 teaspoons red curry paste
1 tablespoon yellow curry powder
1 tablespoon white vinegar
1 tablespoon Bragg's liquid aminos
2 teaspoons agave nectar
2 teaspoons Vogue Cuisine vegetarian soup base dissolved in
2 cups water
2 (13.5 ounce) cans light coconut milk
1 tablespoon dehydrated organic cane juice
2 mangoes, chopped (about 2 cups)
1/2 cup uncooked Texmati light brown rice
3 cups fresh green beans, chopped (about a 10oz bag)

Procedure:

1. Heat the olive oil in a large soup pot. Add the garlic and stir. While the garlic is cooking, add the crushed red pepper, ginger, curry paste and curry powder.
2. Add the Manna Soy Gourmet Meatless Curry Chicken, white vinegar, Bragg's liquid aminos, agave nectar, chicken base, coconut milk, cane juice, mangoes, rice and beans.
3. Simmer for 40 minutes until the carrots are tender and the rice is cooked.

Yield: 8 cups

Nutritional Information (per serving):

Calories: 188
Fat: 6.5g
Carbs: 27g
Protein: 9g

Bombay Potato and Spinach Soup

I just got my bag of organic veggies delivered from the Neighborhood Garden. Included was fresh spinach and mushrooms. I had a craving for Bombay potatoes, but let's face it — while it's a tasty dish it's lacking in protein and nutrients for vegans. I was brainstorming what to add to the Bombay potato when I looked at the spinach and mushrooms — et voila, the Bombay potato soup was born. It took me about an hour in the kitchen tinkering with spices and ingredients to get the right amount of curry flavor without it being overwhelming. The perfect blend of veggies and spices, this soup is definitely on my favorites list. I bought a bag of green chili peppers at the farmer's market this week. One of the chili peppers was turning red — that's the one I used in this gluten-free vegan soup. On a hot pepper scale of 1 to 10, this is probably a 7 or 8, so get the iced water ready!

Prep time: 15 minutes
Cook time: 1 hour

Ingredients:
1 teaspoon olive oil
1/2 onion, diced
1 tablespoon minced garlic
2 teaspoons curry powder
1 teaspoon ground coriander
1 teaspoon garam masala
2 large potatoes, diced
4 teaspoons Vogue vegetarian and vegan seasoning, dissolved in 4 cups of water
1 can Muir Glen organic fire-roasted tomatoes
8 button mushrooms, sliced
1 green chili pepper, finely sliced
1 cup peas
1 cup packed fresh baby spinach
1/2 cup lentils
1/8 teaspoon cayenne pepper
1 bay leaf
Pinch sea garlic powder
1/2 teaspoon turmeric
3/4 cup light coconut milk
1 teaspoon agave nectar

Procedure:

1. Heat the olive oil in a soup pot over medium heat. Add the onion and garlic. Sauté for 5 minutes, until the onions have softened. Add the garam masala, curry powder and coriander. Stir fry for one minute.
2. Add the potato, broth, tomatoes, mushrooms, chili pepper, peas, spinach, lentils, cayenne, bay leaf, turmeric and sea garlic powder in a large saucepan. Bring to a boil and then simmer for 45 minutes.
3. Add the coconut milk and agave. Stir well. Simmer on very low (it should barely bubble) for 10 minutes more. Remove the bay leaf before serving.

Yield: 6 servings (about 1 1/2 cups each)
Nutritional Information (per serving):
Calories: 379
Fat: 6g
Carbs: 65g
Protein: 19g

Fire Roasted Tomato and Vegetable Soup with Spiced Paprika

This delectable soup has a zing of Southwest flavor yet uses a variety of summer vegetables. It was perfect soup for a stormy June night in Florida (courtesy of tropical storm Debby). Actually, this soup came about from leftovers in my fridge. With storm waters rising and roads blocked, there was no way to get out of the house and get to the store. So I opened my fridge, eyed the contents, and wondered what I could make with the left over veggies I had in the drawer. One of the wonderful things I love about creating a new recipe is tasting the soup every ten minutes or so and adjusting the seasonings, or adding a little garlic powder or spice. The potato in the soup actually came about at some point when I realized the soup was a little on the garlic powdery side (a potato counteracts that — a tip I learned from an old Betty Crocker cookbook of days gone by). This gluten-free vegan Southwestern style vegetable soup uses Vogue seasoning and soup base, which I consider indispensable in my kitchen for flavor and convenience. You can probably shorten the cooking time to 20 minutes or so (until the vegetables have softened). My preference is to have soup bubbling on low for at least an hour…sometimes two. The flavors seem to blend better. The extra half cup of water simmers off during the cooking time, so if you choose to simmer for a shorter time, reduce the water by a half cup.

Prep time: 20 minutes
Cook time: 1 hour
Ingredients
1 teaspoon vegetable shortening
1 teaspoon garlic, minced
1 yellow onion, diced
1 small zucchini, diced
1 small yellow squash, peeled and diced
1/2 yellow bell pepper, peeled and diced
1 medium potato, peeled and diced
1/2 cup cooked chickpeas
2 cans Muir Glen fire roasted tomatoes
3 tsp Vogue vegetarian soup base dissolved in 3 1/2 cups water
2 tablespoons Melissa's Soyrizo

1/8 teaspoon hot paprika
1/2 teaspoon oregano
1/4 teaspoon dried cilantro
1/4 teaspoon cumin
Pinch sea garlic powder
Pinch black pepper

Procedure:

1. Melt the vegetable shortening in a large saucepan over medium heat. Reduce to medium low; add the garlic and onion and sauté for 5 minutes, until the onion has softened.
2. Add the zucchini, squash, bell pepper, tomatoes, soup base/water, soyrizo, paprika, sea garlic powder, black pepper, oregano, cilantro and cumin to the pan.
3. Reduce heat to medium low and simmer for at least one hour.

Serves: 5

Nutritional Information (per serving)

Calories per serving: 148
Fat: 2g
Carbs: 29g
Protein: 8g

Slow Cooker Mulligatawny Soup

Mulligatawny literally means "pepper water" in India. This slow-cooker recipe saves a busy day when I don't have time to cook a meal. This gluten-free vegan version of mulligatawny omits the usual meat found in the West (lamb, chicken, or beef) and replaces it with lentils and rice. When I first made this soup I didn't have any tamarind on hand (tamarind is a traditional ingredient in Indian and Thai dishes — it was a sweet/sour flavor). If you do happen to have any tamarind paste on hand, you can omit the lime juice and apricots, replacing them with 1 1/2 teaspoons of tamarind concentrate. If you don't have a slow cooker (although my opinion is that every gluten-free vegan kitchen should!) then sauté the onion and garlic in a soup pan for about 5 minutes until tender, then add the rest of the ingredients (except for the rice). Add the rice at the end, as suggested in the Procedure, and you'll have a deliciously authentic Indian soup. By the way, I was a little lazy today when it came to chopping veggies. Another gadget I can't do without in the kitchen — a food processor. Peel the veggies, throw them in the processor and voila! Instant finely chopped diced veggies. A small warning with soup that contains rice — once you've added the rice, don't let the soup cook too long or the rice will soak up all the water (a lesson I learned a while ago when I let the soup sit for several hours after adding rice — I ended up with mush rice instead of soup!).

Prep time: 15 minutes

Cook time: 7 hours (slow cooker)

Ingredients

1 small yellow onion, finely chopped
2 teaspoons minced garlic
1 teaspoon dried ground ginger
1/2 (4,25oz) can green chile peppers, chopped
1/2 cinnamon stick
1/8 teaspoon ground cloves
2 teaspoons garam masala
1/2 teaspoon ground turmeric
1 bay leaf
2 1/2 teaspoon yellow curry powder
1/2 large carrot, finely chopped
1/4 green apple – peeled, cored, and finely chopped
1 medium potato, peeled and finely chopped
1/2 cup lentils, rinsed, drained
6 teaspoons Vogue vegetarian soup base dissolved in 6 cups water
3 dried apricots, finely chopped
2 teaspoons lime juice
1/2 cup peas
1/2 cup cauliflower, chopped
1 cup coconut milk
1 tablespoon chopped fresh cilantro
1/2 cup rice

Procedure

1. Place all ingredients except coconut milk, cilantro for and rice into a slow cooker. Cook on low for six hours. Add rice and coconut milk one hour before serving.
2. Serve with cilantro garnish.

Serves: 4

Nutritional Information (per serving)

Calories: 517

Fat: 7g

Carbs: 95g

Protein: 20g

Summer Black Bean Soup

A simple warmed gluten-free vegan soup of black beans and tomatoes. What I love about this soup is that it takes less than 5 minutes to put together if you "cheat" and use canned beans. While I do tend to keep canned beans at hand, I almost always use dried beans, soaked the night before. That adds a little prep time, but I'm always thinking ahead when it comes to dinners. If you have kids, trust me — they will love this soup. Or you can even serve it cold (although I've never been able to bring myself to eat cold beans…for some reason my stomach refuses to even consider it!). Serve the soup topped with vegan sour cream, chopped avocado, tomato, cilantro or my crispy gluten-free croutons.

Prep time: 3 minutes

Cook time: 1 minute

Ingredients:

4 cups black beans, cooked

1 10-ounce can Ro*Tel® Original Diced Tomatoes & Green Chilies

1 8-ounce can Tomato Sauce-No Garlic powder Added

1-1/2 cups water

1 teaspoon ground cumin

Procedure:

1. Combine black beans, tomatoes, tomato sauce, water, and cumin in food processor or blender. Blend until smooth (or you can leave it a little chunky if you prefer a chunkier soup).
2. Place in a soup pan and bring to a simmer.

Servings: 6

Nutritional Information (per serving):

Calories: 194

Fat: 4g

Protein: 9g

Carbs: 29g

Cream of Broccoli Soup Recipe with Coconut Milk

Cream of anything soup has to be one of my favorite ways to use up those veggies in the produce drawer. Although I've used broccoli for this gluten-free vegan soup, you can easily replace it with mushrooms, tomatoes, or potatoes. Talking of potatoes, I've found they're a great way to thicken soups, stews and chilies. I keep a box of powdered potato flakes on hand for when I don't want to go through the trouble of peeling and boiling potatoes (which isn't often — I have to admit, I love being in my kitchen!). You can purchase croutons to top the soup off, or you can make your own vegan gluten-free croutons. I recommend making your own to use up that stale gluten-free bread.
Prep time: 20 minutes
Cook time: 25 minutes

Ingredients:
1 Tbsp virgin olive oil
2 cloves of garlic, minced
1/4 cup diced sweet onion
1 tsp grated ginger
1 teaspoon red curry paste
5 cups broccoli florets
3 cups of peeled and diced gold potatoes
1/4 cup chopped fresh parsley
Pinch garlic powder
Pinch black pepper
1 cup coconut milk
Handful of gluten-free croutons
4 tsp vegan sour cream

Procedure

1. Heat the olive oil in a large soup pot over medium heat. Sauté the minced garlic, sweet onion, ginger and curry paste in the olive oil for 1 minute. Add the broccoli and potatoes. Add enough water to just cover the vegetables.
2. Add the chopped parsley, garlic powder and pepper.
3. Bring the vegetables to a boil and then reduce to simmer. Simmer for 20 minutes, covered, until the potatoes are tender.
4. Puree in batches in a blender and then return the soup to the pot. Add the coconut milk and heat gently (do not boil).
5. Serve with a spoon of vegan sour cream and a few croutons.

Serves 4

Nutritional Information (per serving)
Calories: 139
Fat: 5g
Carbs: 21g
Protein: 5g

Gluten-free Vegan: Thai African Peanut Soup

I was first introduced to African peanut soup in 2011 at a local bookstore cafe, Chamblin's in downtown Jacksonville. The manager refused (nicely!) to turn over her secret recipe, so I went on a quest to perfect recipe — it only took me four tries. This gluten-free vegan African peanut soup is infused with Thai curry and fresh jalapeño, so each bite comes with a kick. Packed with protein from beans and peanuts, this filling soup combines spicy with sweet for a dish that is hearty enough for a main course. It's actually more reminiscent of a Thai soup than an African one (probably thanks to the spice), hence the name of the dish. But it's so tasty — who cares about the name?

Prep time: 20 minutes
Cook time: 1 hour 5 minutes

Ingredients

1 Tbsp olive oil
1 Tbsp red Thai kitchen curry paste
1/2 cinnamon stick
1 red onion diced
4 cloves garlic clove minced
1/2 cup peanut butter
1/2 cup water
1 sweet potato peeled and cut into bite size pieces
1 red pepper chopped
1 jalapeño pepper, seeded and chopped
1 can black eyed peas, rinsed and drained
1 can black beans rinsed and drained
1 can white beans drained and rinsed
4 cups vegetable broth made with 4 cups of water and 2 Knorr vegetable bouillon cubes.
1/2 tsp crushed red pepper flakes
1 lime, juiced
1 generous pinch garlic powder
1 generous pinch black pepper
2 Tbsp chopped fresh cilantro

Procedure:

1. Heat the olive oil on medium heat in a large soup pan. Add the curry paste, cinnamon stick, red onion and garlic.
2. Sauté for 3-4 minutes until onions are softened.
3. Boil the water, and then whisk the peanut butter into the water with a fork.
4. Add the peanut butter mixture and all remaining ingredients except for the cilantro into the soup pan.
5. Bring to a boil, reduce heat to simmer, and then simmer for 1 hour.
6. Serve garnished with cilantro.

Recipe note: Knorr vegetable bouillon has sugar in it, so it adds a bit of sweetness to the soup. If you want to use home-made vegetable stock, you'll want to add 1 or 2 tsp of a sweetener like agave nectar to the soup.

Servings: 8

Nutritional Information (per serving)
Calories 664.24
Total Fat 20.41g
Carbohydrates 95.36g
Protein 28.82g / 58%

Photo credits

Apple Crumble: wiennat | Flickr.com
Cupcakes: Kristin_a | Flickr.com
Pizza: jeffreyw | Flickr.com
Multigrain sandwich bread: Grongar | Flickr.com
Vegan flax bread: Francis storr | Flickr.com
French baguette: Jspatchwork | Flickr.com
Garlic herb croutons: Missy and the universe | Flickr.com
Bread with poppy and caraway seeds: editor_B | Flickr.com
Naan: Vortistic | Flickr.com
English Muffin: Stalteri | Flickr.com
Croutons: Lisa Clarke | Flickr.com
Crepes: Vegan Feast Catering | Flickr.com
Chocolate chip banana muffins: t-dubisme | Flickr.com
Danish Pastry: Kochtopf | Flickr.com
Blueberry pancakes: Janineomg | Flickr.com
Hot breakfast cereal: Mccun934 | Flickr.com
Savory vegetable pancakes: Franksteiner | Flickr.com
Meatloaf: chispita_666 | Flickr.com
Shepherd's pie: Harshlight | Flickr.com
Portabello mushroom burger: Girl interrupted eating | Flickr.com
Curry pic by allisonmseward12 | Flickr.com
Tangy stir fry: exfordy | Flickr.cim
Thai curry: Missy and the universe | Flickr.com
Mashed vegetable curry: nSeika | Flickr.com
Vegetable curry: Kirti Poddar | Flickr.com
Potato and chickpea curry: Sleepyneko | Flickr.com
Daal with mashed vegetables: Sonia! The healthy foodie | Flickr.com
Stuffed peppers" Mary Thompson | Flickr.com
"Chicken" curry: Axxylz | Flickr.com
Butter chickpea curry: Dichohecho | Flickr.com
Lentil, Spinach, cashew curry: Mr. T in DC | Flickr.com
Spaghetti and meatballs: Culinary Geek | Flickr.com
Tomato marinara: Naotakem | Flickr.com

Spaghetti Soyrizo: Cyclone Bill | Flickr.com
Bean enchiladas: Edsel L | Flickr.com
Bean and sweet potato enchiladas:
Karenandbrademerson | Flickr.com
Nacho salad" Jeffreyw | Flickr.com
Chili: Sleepyneko | Flickr.com
Falafel: Julesstonesoup | Flickr.com
Falafel burger: vegan feast catering | Flickr.com
10 minute chickpea curry: little blue hen | Flickr.com
Vegetable biryani: Gagandeepsapra | Flickr.com
Pakora: Jeffgun | Flickr.com
Vegan cheese sauce (enchiladas): ilovemypit | Flickr.com
Vegetable bhajis: Mr.T.in DC | Flickr.com
Hummus: Marshall Astor Food fetishist | Flickr.com
Stuffed peppers: sauvehouse113 | Flickr.com
Italian and Pasta soup 2: Stevendepolo | Flickr.com
Italian pasta soup: Rusvaplauke | Flickr.com
Jamaican vegetable soup: Max Braun | Flickr.com
Southwest Soup:www.worththewhisk.com
Bombay potato soup: Iriskh | Flickr.com
Fire roasted tomato soup:emmadiscovery | Flickr.com
Black bean soup: powerskirt:Flickr.com
Broccoli soup: Avlxyz | Flickr.com

CPSIA information can be obtained
at www.ICGtesting.com
Printed in the USA
LVOW01s1025111215
466340LV00019B/254/P

9 781497 399631